Out the Gap

Gabrielle Ní Mheachair

ISBN:0692712496
ISBN-13:9780692712498

To my husband, Keith F. Woeltje

Thanks for your endless patience,
support, and encouragement.

Gabrielle Ní Mheachair

CONTENTS

Gabrielle Ní Mheachair

ACKNOWLEDGMENTS

These tales were previously published episodically in the *Midwest Irish Focus*. Subsequently, they were rewritten and compiled in this book, *Out the Gap: The Donegal Years*. While writing this period of my life, I discovered memory is a fickle and fluid entity. Not only does it change throughout the years, it also mellows or hardens depending on the stuff of one's heart.

Initially, *Out the Gap: The Donegal Years*, was written exclusively from memory. However, the editing process required the verification of dates, times, and event sequences. Hence, I scoured from my original diaries for accuracy. Imagine my consternation when I discovered my memory was not quite as exact as I would have insisted. Event sequences were the most inaccurate aspects of my recollections. I was forced to make a decision: Do I write a memoir or a diary? The choice was easy. This is a memoir. It is how I choose to remember. And I remember with a happy heart.

A special thanks to my sisters, Catherine, Carmel, and Margaret, who allowed me to use their given names! They are proud to have been part of my adventures. All other names are changed to protect identity. Some place names and locations are changed, and in places some physical descriptions are altered.

I would like to thank my daughter Maeve Woeltje and my editor Katie Sharp for editing the final work, and my son John Woeltje who designed the book cover. An additional thanks to my dear friend Ambrose McCreanor, who provided the perfect picture for the front cover!

A final word: All the wonderful people I met in my life have added color and texture to my experiences. They helped mold me into the person I am today. Thank you for being the woven threads in the fabric of my adventurous journey.

THE BISHOP'S HOUSE

When I graduated from college as a qualified primary teacher, there wasn't a job to be had in Ireland. With four colleges churning out up to six hundred teachers a year, the old folks couldn't retire fast enough to accommodate us all! Connections and nepotism seemed the only way to secure a position. Most parishes hired their own, but of course my parish had a policy of not hiring local girls; "too familiar with the families" was their excuse. And of course my father was the wrong political party. I was screwed.

There I was, out on the street, papers in hand, and no job to go to. I applied to hundreds of schools, interviewed at some, and was turned down by all. For six months my depression grew to desperation.

Finally, taking the advice of my good friend Mildred, I applied to schools in Donegal.

England was next door, America across the way, but Donegal was out there somewhere hanging just south of the North Pole. I had never met a soul from Donegal, and no one I knew had ever been there. Only the desperate applied to Donegal. I was desperate.

Daily in undisguised disgust mother threw the mail on the kitchen table, "All fat," she spat caustically.

"Leave 'em there I'll get them later."

On Saturdays I dragged the armchair right up to the fireplace and dumped the box of rejection letters that had accumulated over the week on the floor beside me. I pulled out the curricula vitae to be reused for next week's applications and systematically tossed the rejection letters into the flames. While busy with this weekly ritual, I heard the postman pull up outside the window and engage in polite chatter with Mother. She cut him short rather abruptly and rushed inside all excited.

"It's a thin one," she quipped as she joined me at the fireplace and waited impatiently for me to open it.

"Another fecker who kept my CV and didn't bother to return it!" I snapped. "Just leave it there. I'll attend to it later."

Mother hung over me like an angry teacher, insisting I open it right away.

"Fine, then, I'll open it."

Pulling the envelope apart in one swift motion just for the shock value, I was surprised to find a letter inside inviting me to interview at what we assumed was the bishop's house in Letterkenny, County Donegal. My blood ran cold.

"Letterkenny, where the heck is that?"

"Get the map. Get the map," Mother yelled excitedly.

I got the map and spread it across the floor beside the pile of rescued CVs. There it was, a big red dot, smack dab in the middle of County Donegal. My heart sank. According to the map this town was the larger of only two towns in the whole county. To make matters worse, it was sandwiched between brown mountains and the red border with Northern Ireland.

"Great, I am to be penned in between mortar shells and mountains."

"Well," said Mother, "What are you going to do?"

"What do you mean what am I going to do?"

"Are you going to go for the interview?"

"Are you mad?! I'm not going to Letterkenny. It's at the far edge of the planet. I'll never be seen or heard from again."

"Beggars can't be choosy," she muttered.

"I'll think about it," I agreed, just to avoid a lecture.

When Catherine came home from nursing school that weekend, she was all excited at my news.

"I've never been to Donegal. It'll be a grand adventure."

She began making plans.

"Where ye go I go," Carmel, my younger sister, butted in.

I was seriously miffed. Everyone thought I should go but me.

Mother only wanted rid of me. I was an embarrassment to her, sitting around the house a college graduate with no job. My sisters just wanted "a grand adventure."

Two weeks before the appointed day, we were invited to a twenty-first birthday party in Cork City. Unfortunately it was the night before the interview in Letterkenny.

"Feck that for a racket!" I exclaimed. "We need to leave for Donegal on Friday. It will take us about eight hours to get there. We'll have to spend the night."

"Not at all," Catherine quipped "We can get up early and head for Letterkenny on Saturday morning. The interview isn't 'til six."

"It'll be ten to eleven hours from Cork City," I cautioned.

"Sure, what of it?" said party-happy Catherine. "We can do it."

I really wanted to go to that party. I had just gotten out of twenty-one years of incubation and was sowing all the wild oats I could muster. What's more, Cormack was going to be at the party, and I had plans to dump him. He wanted to settle down, while I was itching for fresh fodder. I phoned the bishop's house and said that it was an awfully long way to go for an interview if the job had already been given. He assured me that all things being equal, I was favored for the job.

"Damn it, I have to go."

On Friday, after subbing all day in a local school, I came home, showered, packed, and got ready to hitchhike to Cork City. Carmel insisted on coming too. I was glad. I hated hitching alone. Mother went ballistic. We politely listened to the thunder for the required amount of time and then left. It took four lifts to get to Cork. At Catherine's flat we changed our clothes and headed off to the Windsor Hotel for the big party. Upon arrival I immediately found a love interest: a cute blond lad with a heart-melting smile sitting all alone at the bar. The challenge was irresistible. While I flirted madly with the young man, Carmel continued to remind me that Cormack would be along at any moment. I bribed her to keep him busy until I had secured myself a follow-up date. She did.

Cormack was tedious at best, and the impatient Carmel soon grew tired of the game. She let him escape, whereupon he attached himself firmly to my side. I was stuck. At some point I managed to excuse myself and took a walk around the hotel, only to find there was another twenty-first party in the ballroom downstairs. The hostess was a college acquaintance of mine. She invited me to join her party. Having spied a cute guy at the bar, I accepted her offer and decided to stay awhile. The guy was as delightful as he was handsome, all dark and brooding with come-to-bed eyes. We flirted outrageously and even took a turn on the dance floor. When he suggested we quit the place and go somewhere less noisy, reality struck. I had to excuse myself, rush upstairs, and check out the status of Cormack and the blond guy.

"I'll be right back," I shouted at handsome. "I just have to let my sister know I'm leaving."

I dashed out of one ballroom and upstairs to the other party.

Reluctantly Carmel returned to entertain Cormack while I reconnected with the cute blue-eyed blond at the bar. Eventually her unforgiving glare warned me that her patience had run thin; it was time to sort myself out, or she was going to blow the whistle. I managed to take her aside and explain that at this point I really needed her, because now there were three guys to entertain, two above and one below. My fifteen-year-old sister was aghast and began lecturing me on my dishonorable behavior.

Having no choice left, I rejoined Cormack but was so curt he left in a huff. Juggling the other two was a blast, and at the end of the night I walked out on both. The two-hour car ride back to Tipperary was sheer punishment with Catherine driving like a crazed maniac, Carmel's tirade droning in my ears, and images of the impending interview swirling in my brain.

The next morning, at some ungodly hour, the alarm went off. It was going to be a long day. Letterkenny was at least eight hours away, and the interview at the bishop's house was at six in the evening. There was no time to waste as we headed into a land where none of us had ever gone before.

Mother insisted I dress for the interview just in case time was an issue. It was an excuse to vet my outfit before I left the house.

"You look great!" she assured me as I unrolled my nylons.

"What are you doing?"

"I hate the feeling of nylons on my legs. I'll pull them back on before the interview, but I'm not wearing them the whole way to Donegal."

"Well don't forget," she warned. "A woman isn't dressed without her nylons."

Catherine arrived downstairs scantily clad in stiletto heels and her hold-all, green leather handbag dangling from her shoulder. Carmel put a beanbag and a blanket in the back of the van for herself.

"Do you have the address, a phone number, money?" Mother asked. "Have you everything now? Take a quick sweep before you leave."

"We're grand, we're grand. This bloody interview! What a darn inconvenience. I'd rather be in bed. I'm so tired," I muttered angrily.

Mother ushered us to the van, lugging the two-foot-tall Lourdes bottle in her arms. She unscrewed the cap and doused us with a handful of holy water. We screamed in shock as the drops of water splatter upon our naked faces. You'd think we were going to America the way she was carrying on and crying and saying things like, "Safe trip. Be careful! Do you have the holy water in the glove box? Are you wearing your miraculous medals? Be sure to say a decade of the rosary on the road."

She stood at the gate and waved us all the way down the driveway until we hit the main road and were hidden from her view.

The trip to Letterkenny was uneventful despite the fact we failed to recite the rosary. We parked at a supermarket. I clamored over the seat into the back where Carmel helped me with the nylons. Catherine did my hair and makeup. By five-thirty I was all dolled up and ready to go.

Finding the bishop's house was easy. It was a fine-cut limestone building in the English style, several stories high with a polished limestone stairs to the first floor. Carmel reminded us that we should park behind the house in case the bishop spotted the van and assumed we were about to rob the place.

"First impressions count," she declared.

Friends and acquaintances fondly called our Toyota LiteAce van the Tipperary Express, while everyone else assumed we were up to no good. It was light blue with two front seats and an empty, windowless back. We covered a lot of Ireland in that van and always had a place to sleep, eat, and party.

The girls turfed me out onto the footpath and drove around the corner. I stood on the pavement, waiting until they were out of sight. With trepidation I climbed the steps toward a pair of massive, ornately carved mahogany doors. I felt like Thumbelina outside the giant's castle.

Do I rap the large brass knockers, or is there a bell? I wondered.

It took a moment to locate the white, modern push-bell hidden on the right between the frame and the stone. A petite, well-groomed elderly lady answered. Her perfect blue-rinse perm gave testimony to a recent hair appointment. With an expectant, welcoming smile her frail frame propped open the heavy door, allowing me just enough breath to slip past her.

"Did you come all this way alone?" she queried.

"Och no. My sisters are waiting in the car."

"Yerra, bring them in! Bring them in, or they'll perish in this cold," she insisted.

I thanked her for her kindness and rushed around back ushering the delighted pair ahead of me. The housekeeper was most gracious and showed us into a large waiting room to the right of a curving staircase matching the hall door. The instant she shut the door behind her, Catherine and Carmel set about the room searching through drawers and behind cabinet doors commenting on everything they saw. Catherine found a closet packed to the gills with printer paper. She grabbed a pack and shoved it into her green bag. "This could come in handy for taking notes."

Carmel, not to be out done, took a fistful of pens and pencils. I glared, stared, and begged them to behave, but they only laughed at me. I hadn't the energy to argue. My stomach was heaving and my mind reeling. I paced the floors, anxiously trying to shut them out. Shortly thereafter a priest summoned me, leaving the girls alone in the room.

The interview panel included the usual string of characters: the parish priest, the principal, a teacher, and one parent. I presented myself well and could only hope for the best. When I left the interview room, the priest followed behind and directed me downstairs to the kitchen.

"The housekeeper is gone home, so I sent your sisters downstairs to fix themselves a cuppa and have something to eat. You'll have a long journey ahead of you," he said kindly before disappearing back into the room.

Below in the kitchen there they were, the pair of them, sitting at the table like royalty and a feast spread out before them.

"This place is great! They have loads of goodies. What will you have?" said Catherine as she jumped to her feet and opened the fridge for me to examine.

"Just a cup of tea. I'm not hungry. My stomach is a mess."

"Mine would be too," said Carmel, as they both exploded laughing.

"What's so funny?"

"Nothing."

"You guys are up to something. I know it."

"Honestly, we're not. But isn't this great! We get to raid the bishop's kitchen?" Catherine added.

"Is there any brown bread?" I asked. "I need something plain on my stomach."

"I'll forage some for you," Catherine coaxed. "Sit down there now and enjoy that cup of tea. You deserve it after all you've been through. Carmel, you start packing up."

"Should we take a few things for the road?"

"Just a bit of fruit," said Catherine as she emptied the fruit bowl into her handbag.

"What about the biscuits?"

"We'll just take a packet or two. Sure the bishop has loads."

"Gee, I'm glad we parked the van out back," grinned Carmel.

"Yea, it's dead handy, just outside the door."

Carmel found a cardboard box in the trash pile and began packing it with whatever tempted her fancy from the cupboards. Catherine tackled the fridge.

"These are bad for the bishop. We're only doing him a favor," Catherine said as she handed off a variety of glass-bottled sodas to Carmel.

"Grab an opener from the drawer while you're at it," Carmel ordered.

"Girls, girls, ye can't do that. It's daylight robbery," I pleaded.

"He told us to take what we wanted, and that's what we're doing!" exclaimed Carmel.

"He didn't mean for you to clean him out of house and home."

"We won't take any furniture!"

"Well there goes any chances of a job," I muttered.

"Don't worry your head about it," Catherine said.

"We've already taken care of that."

"Yea, it's a done deal!" Carmel added.

"What do you mean?"

"While you were interviewing, we found a box of baptismal registration cards and filled them out with your name and address."

"Every single one," Carmel boasted, adding salt to the wound.

"And I filled out the marriage certificates with Cormack as groom and you as bride," Catherine continued. They bent over laughing.

"Why would ye do such a thing?" I whined.

"There's no way in hell you're working in Donegal. The fun's over if you live all the way up here. Cop yourself on. You can't take this job."

"Yea, if you think the Tipperary Express is going from Cork to Donegal via Templemore every weekend, you're mightily mistaken," Carmel added. "Besides, all the parties are in Cork. You're on the wrong point of the compass, dearie."

A very long silence ensued, all the while the girls continued to busy themselves cleaning up and cleaning out. I finished my tea.

"Let's go home," I pleaded. "I'm sick, and I'm tired, and I just want to be on the road."

"Is everything packed up?" Catherine asked Carmel.

"Yep, we're ready for road."

"Grand. So, we're for Strabane."

"Strabane? That's on the other side," I said, in disbelief.

"I know it is," Catherine replied. We're only a few miles from the border, and I have never been in Northern Ireland."

"At this hour of the night? In the van? They'll think we're smugglers or IRA. We'll be shot on sight."

"Not at all. Who'd shoot three girls in a van?" Catherine scoffed.

"Don't you ever listen to the radio? They shoot people up here all the time. It's a war zone! Please, let's just go home."

"Nope! I'm crossing the border whether you come or not. Besides, it's faster to go home through the north. Did you know that?"

When Catherine had her mind set on something, there was no budging it. And if she got into trouble, she counted on me to get her out of it. I had to go along with the plan. We headed for the Camel's Hump at Strabane.

The border crossing outside Letterkenny, affectionately known as the Camel's Hump, is situated on the far side of the river Finn, where a garrison of English soldiers, Royal Ulster Constabulary (RUC), and other military with various colored berets and uniforms monitor the border between Northern Ireland and the Free State. Catherine brazenly drove up to the crossing and stopped as ordered. A tall handsome RUC man asked for her ID and questioned her as to her business in the North. All the while the other uniformed men walked around the van inspecting under and over. Finally, they demanded to inspect the inside. Carmel and I were ill at ease. Catherine, on the other hand, was doing her usual stupid, pretty girl routine.

"License please. What's your business in Strabane?"

"We're going to Five Mile Town to visit a college friend."

"What's her name?"

"Bridget Sullivan. Is that a real gun?"

"Yes, ma'am."

"Can I touch it?"

"No ma'am."

"Oh, my! You have guns on your hips as well! Why do you need all those guns?"

"For protection ma'am."

"Why would a fine, handsome man like you need protection?"

"Ugh, gag me now," whispered Carmel. "Soon she'll be making a date."

"So are you free later tonight?" Catherine asked in response to this rebuke.

"Sorry, ma'am, I'm on duty all night."

"Pity," smiled the flirtatious Catherine.

"Can we go now?" I snapped.

Eventually, we were waved on. At once Carmel and I gave Catherine an ear bashing for prolonging our agony. We were genuinely terrified. There we were, ten o'clock at night, corralled by more military than we had ever seen in our lives, each carrying an arsenal of weaponry ready and willing to use it as they saw fit. We Southerners had heard stories of these guys taking the law into their own hands. Surrounded by vivid reality, I was reluctant to test those theories. Unfortunately Catherine saw all males as a conquest; the armed and uniformed ones were a novelty and particularly appealing.

Once across the border we had no choice but to search for the obscure village of Five Mile Town. It was very late when our van screeched to a halt outside the Sullivan home. Mrs. Sullivan took her time answering our loud knocking. She stepped outside on the flagstone and pulled the door closed behind her. When her eyes swept over the van, her lips stretched into a thin line and her jaw tightened.

"No, Maura is not at home."

"Well, where is she?" we demanded.

"I'm not quite sure. I think she's in town on a date."

"Is she with Ian?"

"I'm not sure."

"Ach, we'll find her. Where is her favorite haunt?"

"She goes to them all."

"We better get going before closing time, or we'll never find her," piped Carmel as she checked the time.

"Nice meeting you misses."
The three of us jumped back into the van and tore up the gravel driveway as we sped out to the main road.

"She wasn't very helpful," said Catherine.

"I bet she thought we were going to kidnap Maura," Carmel added.

"We told her who we were."

"Three respectable farmers' daughters speeding around Northern Ireland at midnight in a LiteAce van with a Southern registration! Would you believe us?" I exclaimed.

The town was small, and we knew we'd have no bother finding her if we split up. Unfortunately, when we hit the outskirts of town, there was a police roadblock waiting for us. By the time we had been interrogated and searched, and put a halt to Catherine's flirting, the pubs were closed and the town empty.

"Let's go home," Carmel suggested.

There was no argument from me. It was late, and there was nothing left to do. Catherine agreed to turn south.

The tarmac was pitch-black. The countryside was pitch-black. The sky was pitch-black. Other than the luminescent white stripe down the middle of the road, there was no light. It was like driving through a dark tunnel with only a broken dotted line to guide us. To make matters worse, there were no road signs, no villages, no houses, and no traffic. We drove for miles through this no-man's land trying to figure out where we were. Eventually we came upon a lighted village with pro-IRA murals all over the place. I was reminded of the warning that Southern vehicles were hijacked and used as burning roadblocks.

"Put your pedal to the metal and don't slow down for anything," I ordered.

Catherine was only too delighted to oblige.

On the far side of town we were plunged back into total darkness. We drove about a mile when suddenly way in the distance we could make out swinging white lights.

"It's the IRA," I wailed. "We're dead."

"What will I do?" Catherine pleaded.

"Speed up and run 'em through," Carmel insisted. Catherine drove for the lights.

Darting military shadows became unmistakable against the blinding spotlights pointed right at us. It was another roadblock.

"It's the police," Catherine screamed as she rammed on the brakes, coming to a screeching halt inches from the barrier. Carmel was jerked forward and banged her head on the back of the driver's seat. My ribs were bruised by the sudden tightening of the seat belt, but Catherine was unscathed, having braced herself for the sudden stop. A dozen gun barrels appeared at the windows. Catherine lowered hers.

"Hi guys, isn't it a lovely night? You wouldn't happen to have a cigarette, would you?"

We were ordered out of the van, our hands up, while a host of camouflaged men crept out of the shadows and set to work searching the van under, over, and through. A couple of guys slid under the car with flashlights to search the chassis. Another pair punched the beanbag, emptied boxes, pulled up carpet, opened glove compartments, the boot and the bonnet. They even rifled our handbags!

"God, maybe the bishop sent them!" I thought for a fleeting second as I nursed my bruised ribcage.

Carmel sat hunched over on the roadside, sobbing into her cupped hands, while Catherine lounged on the beanbag surrounded by admiring officers sharing cigarettes. The commanding officer took me aside for interrogation.

"You do realize, Miss, that if you had run our road block we would have opened fire."

Oh, God! I had no idea. I knew this trip North would all end in trouble.

"We're from Templemore," I said, hoping it would ring a bell, the Garda Barracks and all that.

The guy just glared at me with depthless eyes and a straight face. I could tell he was trained to mistrust the world. Nothing I said impacted his rigid, stone face. Fortunately, it didn't take him long to figure out that we were exactly who we said we were: three stupid, lost, Southern girls.

After a long silence he suggested, "Miss, I think for your own safety you should follow us to the border."

The soldiers promptly reloaded the van and escorted us to the nearest official crossing. Before they waved us off, the commanding officer came to the driver's window and strongly recommended we never return.

"You have been reported and recorded, you know!"

The cross border soldiers couldn't have been more accommodating, thanks to our armed escorts and Catherine's flirting. We were an interesting diversion for the all-night patrol.

"All those fine bodies!" Catherine sighed. "We simply must come back!"

Carmel and I locked eyes in agreement of our disagreement.

THE GOOD SAMARITAN

"Gabrielle, it's your turn to drive. I'm exhausted," Catherine announced once we were safely in the Free State. She climbed into the back with Carmel, and I drove.

"I'm a little peckish, Carmel. Do we have any food left?"

The crinkling of chocolate wrappers, the munching of biscuits, and the crunching of apples resonated from the back of the van as my sisters proceeded to picnic on their stolen goodies.

Driving puts me to sleep, and it wasn't long before I began to doze at the wheel.

"Catherine," I begged, "I simply can't keep my eyes open. Will you take over for a while?"

"Nope! I drove all day long and now it's your turn. Here, have an apple. It'll keep you awake."

I forged on. Suddenly, as if from nowhere, I was transported into a world of huge, soft, juicy snowflakes fluttering around me like plucked feathers floating in the breeze. The girls were fast asleep on the beanbag unaware of the blizzard conditions enveloping us. Exercising every ounce of energy to concentrate on the road, it wasn't long before I was emotionally and physically drained and had to pull over for a wee nap. While I napped, the heavens dumped truckloads of snow on the countryside. I managed to pull the van back onto the road, but it was almost impossible to navigate through the dense curtain hanging before me. I slipped and skidded on turns, four-way crossings, hills, and stops. Outside Athlone, two hours from home, my nerves failed me. Once again, I pulled over.

"Catherine, wake up. It's snowing and I keep skidding off the road. You'll have to drive."

Catherine was awake in an instant and without argument took the wheel. I tried to catch some sleep in the front seat beside her but was jarred awake by her screaming every time she did a three-point turn. Soon, we found ourselves dangling over a ditch.

"Get out the pair of you and push," she ordered.

"But I'm in nylons and high heels!" I protested.

"We can hang here all night, fall into the ditch, and drown, or ye can push us out."

"Fine so."

With great effort Carmel and I pushed the van back on the road.

Blizzard conditions continued. At Birr, one hour from home, we got stuck on a hill. Once again we were ordered out and miraculously managed to shove the van up the hill. Soon we were plowing our way through the worst snowstorm to hit Ireland in ten years. On the far side of Roscrea there was another hill.

"Out ye get," Catherine commanded.

"We're getting good at this. Looks like we'll be pushing it all the way home," Carmel jibed.

"Why can't she get out and push?" I complained. "My legs are frozen solid."

"Leave well enough alone. If she gets thick she'll drive off and leave us," Carmel cautioned.

We pushed and shoved, prayed and cursed, but it was no use. The van refused to take the hill. It actually slid backward, forcing us down the hill with it. After three attempts, I quit.

"What are we to do now?" Catherine bellowed, as if the weather conditions were our fault.

"We could go the back road," I suggested.

"I don't know any back roads."

"We could take the Dunkerrin Road. I hitched it all last month when I subbed in the school."

"Are you sure there are no hills on it?"

"It's all twists and turns, but the hills are only bumps compared to this one. We should be fine."

"Grand so. It seems we have no choice anyway."

Catherine spun the van without difficulty and following my directions we started for home via the Dunkerrin Road. All was well till we came to the foothills of the Devil's Bit Mountain. There the road began to dip and rise in little low knolls. It wasn't long before our luck ran out and we found ourselves stuck in a snowdrift filling a hollow between two rises. The van sank into the snow and spun a little on the spot before pulling us into the ditch. We were trapped between a three-foot snowbank and a mucky ditch only thirty minutes from home.

"We're stuck fast," said the wise Carmel.

"I can see that," snarked Catherine.

"It's pitch-dark and the middle of the night. I'm taking a nap. We can figure out our bearings in the morning," I suggested.

Everyone agreed this was a good idea. Catherine and I climbed into the back of the van where the three of us snuggled up tight for what was left of the night.

Chilling cold and biting damp woke us.

"Turn on the van and heat us up," Carmel begged.

"Why didn't you think of that before," Catherine said testily. She was losing her cool and getting quite witchy with us.

The three of us climbed into the front seats and huddled close to the heater.

"Someone will have to come this way eventually and rescue us," Carmel added in an effort to cheer us up.

"Who in their right mind would be out on a morning like this?"

"This is farmer country. They have to milk the cows."

"I don't see any cows anywhere," Catherine announced sarcastically.

"They're in barns or sheds waiting to be milked."

"And what about the creamery run? Don't they have to take the milk to the creamery?"

"Actually, now that you say it, that's what bulk tanks are for, and they don't run on Sundays!"

"Looks like we'll be here a while then," I said. "Today is Sunday."

With a clatter and a clunk the engine died.

"What just happened?" asked Carmel timidly.

"No petrol left to run the engine or the heat," Catherine guffawed in despair.

"What are we going to do now?"

"Well, you and Carmel are going to go out there and look for help, or else we can all sit here and freeze to death."

"We're not dressed for plodding miles in this weather," I protested.

"Well someone has to go, and it's not going to be me. I'm staying with the van. It's my van after all."

Reluctantly, Carmel and I climbed out of the van and trudged slowly through the deep snow for about a mile until we came to a small cottage tightly wrapped in weeds and overgrown bushes.

"It looks abandoned to me."

"We may as well knock."

We knocked, we banged, we shouted, we yelled, but to no avail. It was an abandoned cottage.

"We could shelter here?"

"We're as well off in the van," I replied.

"I suppose," Carmel muttered unconvinced.

"It's easier to stay warm in the van, it's smaller and enclosed."

"But we could light a fire and keep ourselves warm in the cottage?"

"Do you plan on gathering firewood? Cause I don't."

"Now what?"

"Back to the van."

"Catherine will go wild if we go back without help."

"My feet are freezing cold. I can hardly feel them. I'm not going further down the road. Besides the next house down that road," and I pointed for effect, "is the haunted one, where the man hung himself from the window! I'm not going near that place."

As we trudged back the mile of road, my feet went completely numb. I couldn't feel them and had difficulty bringing them with me. It seemed like they had died at the knees. Carmel had to half-drag half-carry me back to the van.

When we returned without any sign of help, Catherine yelled at us.

"I can't feel my feet," I challenged. "What do you want us to do, magic a house and help?"

"You probably have frostbite. If you don't warm them up soon, you'll lose your legs," she said matter-of-factly.

I began to cry. Carmel pulled my feet into her lap and tugged at my shoes. They were stuck fast to my swollen feet. I winced in pain as she practically unscrewed my shoes from each foot.

"Pull off those wet tights. They're not helping," she ordered.

I did, and she set about blowing and rubbing my feet trying to bring feeling back into them. Through my tears I muttered, "Carmel I'm hungry. Do you have any food left?"

She rummaged through the bags and the boxes, and pulled out a trio bar.

"This is all we have left. We should have taken that fruit cake," she complained to Catherine.

"You're the one who said leave it, because no one would eat it."

"Well, I'd eat it now if I had it."

"One trio bar is all that's left after all the stuff you took from the bishop's house?" I stammered in despair.

"Yep, we ate the lot while you were driving. You ate some of the fruit yourself."

"But that's all I had to eat in two days, a couple of bits of fruit. That trio bar should be mine. You guys ate the rest of the food."

"Nope," interjected Catherine. "We'll split it three ways. There are three squares, one each."

So the three-inch trio bar was split into three.

Carmel ate hers nibble by nibble and laughed, "If this is my last meal on Earth. I'm going to enjoy it."

I began to cry again—not just because I was hungry and cold, but because my feet were beginning to thaw and the pain was excruciating. There we were, three girls in a van: Catherine in her sullen mode ready to snap anyone's head off, I sobbing in pain, and Carmel giddy on anxiety.

"The *Tipperary Star* headlines will read, 'Three sisters die of exposure trapped in a blue LiteAce van on the Dunkerrin Road,'" she scoffed.

"It's not funny," Catherine retorted.

"I wonder which of us will die first?" Carmel continued unfazed. "Catherine, you have the least body fat. So, you'll go first."

"Nope, it will probably be Gabrielle; she's already weakened with hunger and frostbite, and she is the smallest."

My tears spilled again.

"What will we do with her if she dies?" Carmel asked. "Will we eat her like they do in the movies?"

"Don't be ridiculous, Carmel! We'll just put her out in the snow. I don't want her smelling up the van."

"Would ye mind not discussing my fate in front of me?" I whined. "It's not funny."

"Good point," Carmel agreed, "but at least I have the comfort of knowing that I'll be the last one to go, and with the pair of you gone I'll actually have a chance at survival."

"Carmel, come here," Catherine interrupted.

"What?'

"Come here, look!"

Carmel roughly shoved my feet off her lap and clamored into the front seat beside Catherine.

"I think I see something coming in the distance, do you?"

"You're right, it looks like a car."

Suddenly, and in unison, the pair of them began screaming.

"We're saved. We're saved!"

They pumped up and down in the front seats, rattling the whole van and increasing my leg pain. I was not amused.

"We're saved," they repeated excitedly.
Soon we would be sitting at home by the fire with mother fussing over us savoring warm tea and toast. This terrible ordeal would finally be over.

We sat in patient silence watching that tiny green speck in the distance gradually grow to a full-size tractor. It slowed and pulled alongside the van. We could see a middle-aged woman standing against the opposite door of the tractor. The farmer sitting in the middle leaned toward the window and slid it open. Carmel rolled down the van window.

"Terrible morning?" he greeted.

We stared at him dumbfounded. Of course it was a terrible morning! It had been a terrible morning for hours.

"Is there a problem?" he continued.

"We're stuck," said Catherine as she leaned across Carmel's lap in an effort to get some communication going.

"Lord, that's a divil now isn't it?" the farmer flippantly replied.

"Jack, we'll be late for Mass!" his wife rebuked. Jack took one look at his watch and then at the wife. He realized he had better get moving.

"We better go so," he said.

He slammed the window shut and drove off, never once looking back.

Catherine almost exploded in temper.

"Wait, wait! Look, there's another tractor coming," Carmel interrupted excitedly.

"What do you bet they're going to Mass too?" I added sarcastically.

"Where else would they be going at this hour?" Catherine snapped

The tractor decelerated as it drew near to us. Once more we perked up in hopeful anticipation of salvation. This tractor had a lady and a youth scrunched up against the opposite door, while the farmer had his dog on his side. He leaned toward the window and with difficulty managed to force the mud-encrusted windowpane open.

"Whoa, he's not bad," I muttered from behind. "I'd prefer be rescued by him. Looks like he's got a fine body."

"I saw him first," Carmel shot back.

"You saw the tractor first. You can have that. I get the man inside."

A handsome man was all Catherine needed to switch from crazed maniac to frivolous flirt.

"Morning ladies, is there a problem?"

"Yes, we're stuck fast. Can you help us?"

The handsome farmer turned to look at the woman in the cabin. Her reply was blurred from us by the thickly caked, mud-spattered cab.

"We're out of luck girls," whispered Carmel. "It's obvious that the wife's having none of it."

"How do you now it's the wife?" I asked.

"Wife, kid, farmer, it couldn't be more obvious. Besides any respectable, single, hot-blooded male would jump at the chance to rescue three damsels in distress. It's a wife all right."

Catherine continued her conversation with the farmer.

". . . and then the van got stuck, and we ran out of petrol, and we're freezing cold and starving with the hunger . . ."

All the while she flashed her wide smile and fluttered her eyelashes.

"Well, it looks like you'll need a tractor to tow you out," the cute farmer replied.

"Looks like she's got him," Carmel muttered triumphantly.

"I'll tell ye what girls, we'll get ye out of there when we get back from Mass."

"The wife," Carmel grunted, "she'll make him go home another route, you'll see. We're stuck."

The tractor revved up and trundled off down the road. We were gob smacked.

"What kind of Catholics are ye?" Catherine yelled after them, shaking her fist out the window for effect. "Haven't ye ever heard the story of the good Samaritan?"

"I guess Mass is more important than rescuing us," I muttered.

We then began a discussion about how people are slaves to Mass and rituals but fail to see charity when it is in plain sight.

"I can see the news headlines now," Carmel mused. "Families rush to Mass while three teenage girls freeze to death on the roadside!"

"It'll serve them right to be so shamed," added Catherine. "How far is the church anyway?"

"It'll take them thirty minutes to get there from here, an hour at Mass, and thirty minutes to get back to us. They'll be back in two hours," I calculated.

"They'll be longer than that. They'll stop to gossip outside the church for half an hour, then go into town and buy the newspaper and sweets for the child, and then chat some more, and then back home. I'd say we're in for a three-hour wait," Carmel conjectured.

"She's right," I agreed.

"I'll never last that long," Catherine grumbled.

"Well, there's nothing for us to do but sit tight and hope the first tractor comes back this way and gives us a tow. The wife will never let the second lad back this way."

Three hours later we were tucked under the blanket in the back of the van trying to keep warm. "I hear a tractor," Catherine piped up excitedly.

"Which one is it?"

"The red one."

"It's the fine body. Gabrielle, wake up, the fine body is coming back to rescue us."

I awoke frozen solid and in no mood for chatter. My stomach had sharp pains stabbing through it, my head ached, and my feet burned. I couldn't care less who was coming to rescue us. I yanked the blanket over my head and laid back down.

The tractor eased alongside and stopped. Mr. Fine Body jiggled the mud-caked window open and gestured for us to open ours.

"I'll be back in thirty minutes to get you out, but I must take the Mother home first," he yelled with a great big smile.

"Mother!" said Carmel. "We're in luck."
I started crying. "Another thirty minutes. I can't take it anymore."

"Wait," Catherine yelled at him before he slammed the window shut. "You don't happen to have a cigarette?"

"Sorry, I'm a pipe smoker," he replied.

"A pipe smoker," Carmel repeated with glee. "Wow! Don't you just love a pipe smoker?!"

"He's all yours, Carmel," I muttered disinterested.

"Don't worry, Carmel, I'll get him for you," Catherine assured her.

"No, you won't," Carmel retorted angrily. "We all know what that means."

"I don't know what you're talking about," Catherine snapped.

"You steal all our boyfriends on the guise you are getting them for us. And we don't take secondhand merchandise," I interjected.

"Exactly," Carmel agreed, "so hands off, he's mine."

"We'll see," Catherine said with that devious smile of hers.

An hour later the red tractor returned. A blue one followed. Our fine pipe-smoking friend introduced himself and then introduced his brother.

"One each," Carmel whispered under her breath, assuming I was not interested.

With great speed the pipe smoker ushered all three of us into the cab of his tractor. He drove two miles down the road and pulled into the front yard of a small whitewashed cottage. An elderly couple greeted him at the door. They invited us inside to join them at the fire while the lady of the house cooked the finest breakfast I have ever eaten. We sat at the table like hungry dogs and ate the place clean. Then we returned to the fireside and chit-chatted with our hosts.

"Where's the other one?" Carmel muttered referring to the brother.

"No idea."

As we pondered his whereabouts, the handsome brother drove into the yard with the van in tow. Our rescuer jumped to standing and announced, "Right so, we must get you girls home. I called your mother and she's expecting ye."

"I'll go with the van," said Carmel, hoping to get a leg in with the brother.

"I'll go with you," I said, noticing there was already a connection between the other two. Carmel's glares were enough to refreeze me.

When we arrived home, Mother was standing at the top of the driveway, snow curling down around her. She was crying her eyes out and cradling the plastic Lourdes bottle in her arms.

A VERY IMPORTANT PERSON

No doubt—and as expected—two weeks later I got a letter from the bishop's house saying something along the lines of, "We regret to inform you that we have found a more suitable candidate for the position of Assistant Teacher . . ."

"Of course they found a more suitable candidate!" I raged. "Thanks to my sisters, they think we're a family of deranged kleptomaniacs."

"Now, Gabrielle, it's an ill wind that doesn't blow some good," said Mother encouragingly as I returned to the Saturday burning.

Because convent schools were always hiring new teachers, I decided to visit my aunt, Sister M (Sister Mary). Perhaps she could help.

It took almost a day to hitchhike to her remote and secluded convent. With great trepidation I knocked on the looming wooden double doors that shut these women away from the taint of regular life.

A tiny nun, almost a hundred years old, answered. When she heard who I was, she smiled broadly, welcomed me inside, and escorted me into an elaborately decorated parlor where a coal fire blazed. Three bells summoned Sister M to the room. We were left alone for about an hour before another nun knocked on the door and tentatively pushed herself inside. Bowing like a waiter, she moved into the room, apologizing profusely for the interruption, then busied herself setting the table with real china dishes, glittering silverware, and solid-silver teapots. A sumptuous five-course meal was served over a period of two hours. I felt like a queen being waited on hand and foot.

Sister M and I caught up on the family gossip before eventually discussing the topic dearest to my heart: my unemployment situation and my options. She had no sway with her convent, because their graduates always got the jobs, unlike my parish where they were systematically turned away. All the while we chatted, a willowy blond nun stood silently to one side ready to top my teacup and replenish my plate as they emptied. When we had finished the meal, the blond nun cleared the dishes and left us alone to continue our conversation. As much as Sister M cared for me, there was nothing she could do to help. I understood her position and left the convent still respectfully her dearest niece, but totally crestfallen at my pitiful situation.

About a week later I got a phone call from a nun at my aunt's convent. She was delightful on the phone and suggested that she may have a job lead for me. She would call me back in a week. I was thrilled. I assumed my aunt had put in a good word for me, and perhaps the other nuns in the convent were now scouting out the job market for me. Things were looking up!

A week later, as promised, Sister Attracta phoned. Indeed, she had a lead on a job for me. I was to meet her on Saturday at one o'clock outside Roches Stores, a well-known Limerick City landmark. From there she was going to take me to meet a very important person who could almost guarantee me a job. I was ecstatic and agreed to the meeting without a second thought.

When my sister came home that evening, I told her my exciting news.

"What? You have to be in Limerick City at one on Saturday!" she exclaimed.

'It's a chance at a job," I retorted.

"Well, we've been invited to a twenty-first party on Friday night in Cork. How are you going to be in two places at once?" she demanded to know.

"Shoot! That's typical of my luck."

"Call the nun and reschedule."

"I can't do that."

"You'll have to. I told Ciarán you'd be there, and he's looking forward to meeting you."

"Great, an evening with Ciarán, the fine body— and my latest love interest—or a morning with a nun!"

I called the nun. "Sister Attracta, I just discovered that I have a previous engagement Saturday morning. Can we reschedule?"

"I'm afraid not," she said in that official nunlike voice that almost withers your soul.

"Oh," I responded.

"This important person can only make it on Saturday. It's all arranged. You'll simply have to be at Roches Stores at one." My brain raced. *What if my aunt was pulling strings for me? What if I let her down? What if this is the opportunity of a lifetime? What if. . .?*

"I'll be there, but my sister will be with me. I'll have to hitchhike."

"That's no problem at all. We'll see the pair of you on Saturday," she responded with a sickly, sweet, insincere voice. So typical! Those nuns could go from savage to sweet in one sentence! That's how they always get their way.

Catherine was none too pleased about my decision.

"What was I to do?" I asked her. "She got really bitchy with me. And God knows I need a job."

"You have to go to that party" she demanded. "You can hitch to Limerick Saturday morning."

"I suppose I have no choice," I replied. "Carmel and I will need to be on the road early Saturday if we want to make Limerick by one."

'I wouldn't worry about a lift. You'll have the pick of the trucks from Mitchelstown," she assured us.

"Yea, but we have to get to Mitchelstown first," Carmel interjected sarcastically.

Friday evening after school Carmel and I hitched to Cork City for the party.

Between the pair of us, Catherine and myself, everyone we knew was turning twenty-one. The celebrations were becoming monotonous: the same faces, the same crowd, the same routine. We tried to spice things up by hitting on different guys each time. Of course Ciarán proved a total disappointment. There was no denying he was a handsome hunk with a fine body to boot, but I have no tolerance for slobbering drunks pawing all over me like filthy, grizzly bears. He definitely wasn't worth the long cold trip and sleepless night!

Bleary eyed and tired, Catherine yanked us out of bed before she headed off for work. There was no food in the flat, so we skipped breakfast and trudged through a fresh snowfall to the outskirts of the city. There we stood muffled tightly in scarves, gloves, and thick woolen coats while biting, icy winds tried to hack off our noses and ears.

"Why is it we seem to attract the very worst weather whenever we hitchhike around Ireland?" Carmel asked.

"I don't know. Maybe God's trying to tell us something!"

"In that case, we're very slow learners," she quipped.

"After last night, I'm giving up parties, and hitchhiking, for good," I sighed.

"I wish you had a job and could buy your own car," she said. "Then we could travel in style."

"Dream on girl! Now remember," I cautioned, "be on your best behavior when we meet this nun.

No smart mouthing, no snickering—in fact, just sit quietly and let me do all the talking. Promise!"

"I promise to sit quietly and let you do all the talking," she repeated earnestly.

"Good. If you don't, you're never coming to another place with me again," I warned.

"I always keep my promises, so, you have nothing to worry about."

There is something about bad weather that makes truck drivers speed past hitchhikers. Maybe they're afraid to skid to a halt on the icy roads, or they don't want to open the door and let all that cold air inside. Maybe they resent soggy hikers wetting their cozy cabs, or maybe they just don't see them in the dark, wet surroundings. Whatever the reason, bad weather makes for bad hitchhiking, and we were at high risk of never making it to Limerick in time. A hundred trucks later, an icy heart and panic in my soul, a car pulled up beside us.

"I'm only going up the road a couple of miles," the nice elderly man proffered.

"Grand," said Carmel, "at least we'll get to thaw out a bit."

He let us out in the middle of nowhere and disappeared down a long country lane with grass growing where a stripe should have been. Choking back tears, I stared at my watch, trying to calculate time past and time forward. Our quest was futile.

"We'll never make it! Another job opportunity lost!"

"Well, at least we got to thaw out for a while," Carmel said before interrupting herself. "Hold it, hold it, this truck is slowing down. Yep, it's a lift. You get in first," she squealed in delight.

Whenever we hitchhiked around Ireland I was always the one who had to sit in the front seat or beside the driver in the lorries. Catherine and Carmel assumed I was up and ready to stab them to death with my little keychain penknife if they tried anything. Fortunately, the occasion never presented itself, thought we did have a scare with the flasher! Twice!

We climbed into the warm cab. A kind-hearted driver announced he was going all the way to Limerick and would drop us off down the road from where we needed to be.

"Praise be the Lord!"

True to his word, the trucker dropped us off on the dock road. We almost ran the two blocks to Roches Stores. Having no idea of the protocol from this point forward, we tucked ourselves under the awnings blowing warmth into our frost-fried fingers and doing tippy-toe exercises to prevent our toes from freezing. It wasn't long before a black car pulled alongside us and out popped the nun.

"Yoo-hoo, over here," she cooed.

I immediately recognized her as the willowy, blond tea server from my visit to Sister M. She was charmingly friendly and ushered our frozen bodies into the back of the car. A tall, slim, blond man with a striking resemblance to the nun was at the wheel, while his short, frumpy, dark-haired wife sat in the passenger seat. We three sat in the back. Carmel and I were squashed together in an effort to allow Sister

Attracta ample room. She began chattering about the awful weather. No one seemed to be listening to her. Neither were we. My brain was numb, but Carmel's wasn't. Now and again she gave me that look. I refused to be taunted by her. On some level she seemed to be enjoying herself like she knew something I didn't. Packed into the small car we left Limerick City. After thirty-five minutes the driver pulled to a stop at a well-kept semidetached house in the middle of the romantic lakeside town of Killaloe. We were ushered into a kitchen-come-living room where a warm turf fire awaited us. Formal introductions ensued. The tall, blond man, our driver, was the man of the house; a very pretty woman wearing an apron and in the throes of cooking, was his wife. The frumpy lady, whom we thought the wife, was in fact a sister. I scanned the room for the very important person who was going to give me a job. He wasn't there. Perhaps the bad weather had delayed him!

At the first opportunity, Carmel and I pitched ourselves into the fireside seats desperate to thaw our icy bodies. The others abandoned us and congregated in the hallway, making some commotion about the missing guest. Sister Attracta seemed quite agitated by the absence of Tom. The others assured her he was on his way.

"Ah, ha," I relaxed, "the priest is on his way."

I leaned into the back of the seat, my mind conjuring an informal interview with their relative, Father Tom, presumably the chairman of the school board, and subsequently the man to make me a job offer.

"Tea's up," announced the pretty housewife.

Carmel and I were served where we sat with mountains of goodies piled high on the end tables. I was thrilled with the tea, but my ever-nervous stomach was a mess. Carmel, on the other hand, made a pig of herself, swallowing one pastry after another like she had never been fed a morsel in her whole life.

"Cop yourself on," I hissed through a gritted smile.

"I'm starving!" she mouthed back and continued to stuff her face. I was mortified. As per usual, here she was again, letting me down with a bang.

You can't take her anywhere!" I thought. *I really should travel alone.*

While Carmel gorged and I sipped, the family busied themselves setting the dining room table for a large meal. All the while they chit-chatted with the pair of us. The conversation began with the awful weather. Then it drifted to our family, the Mahers.

"How's your mother? She's a great woman. I don't know how she does it all. So many children and all a credit to her," Sister began.

"And what is it your father does?" the frumpy sister asked.

"He's a farmer and a politician," I replied.

"Oh," she intoned, dying to know what party but not daring to ask.

"Don't worry, dear," the nun added, having noticed her dilemma. "He's the right color. Isn't he?" She smiled at me.

"I suppose," I replied wanting to avoid politics at all cost. Party politics was probably why I was unemployed in the first place.

"Is the oldest at all interested in politics?" the nun continued.

"No, he's a farm manager with no interest whatsoever in politics. He's too busy with his girlfriend."

"Girlfriend?"

"A lovely girl from Galway! We're hoping for an engagement later this year."

"Och, wouldn't that be lovely," the nun agreed with a great big smile on her face.

"What about the second son?" she continued.

"He's in Saudi Arabia."

One by one the credentials of the older siblings were listed, accounted for, and approved upon. Suddenly the doorbell rang.

"The priest," I sighed inwardly and gave Carmel a look of relief.

There she was sprawled out in the oversize arm chair like a scrap-fed pig content to swell and die in her own shit. She returned my look with that knowing smirk still etched across her sassy face. Sister flurried to the door, insisting on opening it herself.

"Tom, Tom, you made it! I was so worried about you. Thank God you're here! Come in, come in!"

She didn't even let him draw breath or take his coat off. The poor man was shoved into the kitchen and planted squarely in our direct line of vision. A huge square block of a man stared from dull, empty eyes at us. When he managed, with much difficulty, to unwrap his overcoat from those expansive shoulders, I noticed there was no priest collar. My heart sank.

"He's not the priest," I grumbled.

The hulky man was introduced to us as Tom. He grunted in reply and reached into his chest pocket to pull out a large, crumpled white handkerchief to wipe his sweating brow. He began tugging awkwardly at his jacket like one who was not used to dressing up. His necktie was pulled too taut and the shirt stretched across his belly gaping at the buttonholes, while the pant legs settled into a neat pile of folds over the caps of his well-polished black shoes. It was obvious he had just marched off the farm into a brand-new untailored suit and driven straight here. He probably had to milk the cows first.

"Dinner is served," the woman of the house announced.

Initially this announcement was politely ignored. Then the nun, who was giddy as a kid goat since the arrival of Tom, reiterated, "Come now, don't be shy, dinner is served."

Carmel leapt to her feet ready to devour plates and all. Sister halted her in her tracks and began assigning seats. I was to sit beside Tom. Carmel was opposite me. Sister was at one end of the table with the house owner at the opposite head. When everyone was settled according to Sister's plan, Carmel kicked me under the table and nodded toward Tom. I glared back warning her to behave. She graced me with a grand grin that blocked a laugh out loud.

Dinner conversation revolved around my credentials. Being a good Catholic girl from a prominent family was top of the list. When they mentioned that I was very sensible girl, with a good head on my shoulders, a nondrinker, and a nonsmoker, Carmel almost spat her food across the table. She took a fit of choking, and every one rallied to rescue her from near death.

"I swallowed my water the wrong way," she confessed most convincingly.

"There, there, you're fine now. Would you like more water?" Sister asked.

"No thank you," she smiled demurely.

I decided to ignore Carmel and remained sitting bold upright, afraid to put a foot out of place, still anticipating the arrival of the very important person that everyone else seemed to have forgotten about. The conversation reverted back to the merits of my existence.

"Gabrielle, your family must be so proud of you graduating from college as a primary school teacher. Teaching is in the family isn't it?"

"It is surely," I said, embarrassed at being the continued focus of conversation.

I could feel my ears burning red and my face turning a bright pink. My stomach knotted like wrung laundry. Yet, every time I sneaked a peak at

Carmel, she was grinning widely and nodding her head in Tom's direction, trying to get me to look at him. Sister ragged on about our huge farm and how we all had to row in to help out.

"Gabrielle, is no stranger to hard work," she boasted to the table. "That family all worked the farm, didn't they, Gabrielle?"

"Absolutely, we all had to do our share," I agreed with a polite smile. I had to remind myself not to prattle on. My brain rehearsed mother's old cants, "Little said is easily mended. Don't give people too much information."

Again Carmel kicked me under the table, grinning like a delinquent monkey and nodding toward Tom. It was hard to appreciate that she was keeping her promise to sit quietly and let me do all the talking when her nods, grins, giggles, and under-the-table kicks were getting on my nerves.

"Lord, sure, you're a great family altogether, and a credit to your parents."

It seemed that Sister Attracta had concluded the list of my fine qualities. Now it was Tom's turn. Everyone turned toward him as Sister began telling us how wonderful he was. He had a good-size farm and a two-story house on a hill with slates. The bathroom was being built as we spoke. He had all his own hair and all his own teeth. He too was a nondrinker and nonsmoker.

"Isn't that right, Tom?"

"Aye," he replied with a grunt.

"Tom's a dairy farmer like your family. He has twenty cows milking daily," she boasted.

Dairy farming meant nothing to me. We got out of cows a few years ago and were now dry-stock and tillage, but I wasn't about to tell her that. Anyway, I wasn't interested in Tom's qualifications. I was anxiously awaiting the priest's arrival.

"All Tom needs now is a wife. Isn't that right Tom?" Sister continued.

Poor Tom, his nose went bright red and the blood rushed toward his ears, which appeared to sizzle. He tugged on his tie, trying desperately to loosen it, but only pulled it tighter. He attempted to struggle out of his dinner jacket and almost toppled the chair in the process. Sister Attracta jumped to her feet and helped him peel the thing off. She hung it on the back of the door and returned to the table. Tom's chair screeched and scraped along the floor as he tried to shuffle it back under the table and return to his meal. Carmel kicked me again! I failed to see the humor. I felt sorry for the poor man.

Not long after, the aproned wife began clearing the dishes. Her husband joined her. The aunt got busy organizing an array of desserts—butterfly buns, biscuits, sponge cake slices, a sherry trifle, and a large mouth-watering chocolate cake—all lined up across the table like a confectionary window. I checked my watch and wondered when on Earth the very important person was going to show up. Perhaps he was coming for dessert? I glanced across the table at Carmel. She was already in motion grabbing desserts from every tray. Her plate was piled high with one of everything. I was livid with her disgraceful lack of respect for these people who were being so kind and generous, and who had only my best interests at heart.

How much food can she put away anyway? I wondered angrily. I just knew she'd puke her guts out the moment the priest showed up. That's just my kind of luck. Tea and cakes, more tea and cakes, and more tea! Soon I was desperate for the little girl's room.

Having grown up in rural Ireland, we had been trained never to ask our host for the bathroom. Many people still had none, and it was important not to belittle or embarrass them. But this was a modern house and was certain to have a bathroom. So, with much trepidation, I begged leave to use the bathroom.

"Top of the stairs!" Sister chirped.

Off I went, glad to have a bit of peace and quiet. I was in no hurry to get back and stalled for as long as I could, hoping that Carmel would follow me. She was well due a piece of my mind. But she was too clever for that! When I eventually sauntered downstairs, I was surprised to find Sister standing at the bottom waiting for me. Guilt flooded my consciousness. Did she think I was robbing the place? I was clean as a whistle. I hadn't even taken the toilet roll. Sheepishly, I made the last few steps toward her. She reached out to place her hand on my shoulder. I flinched. She withdrew and smiled back. When I hit ground level, she set her hand firmly on my shoulder and steered me into the living room.

"We need to chat. Alone!" she whispered.

Totally taken by surprise, I eased ahead of her and stopped in the middle of the room, turning to gape at her like a painted marionette.

"Sit down. Sit down," she ordered in that saccharine voice people use when they are trying to coax you to do something you really don't want to do. I sat down and surveyed my surroundings. It was a typical sitting room situated at the front of the house with a expansive shop window looking out on the street. No cars buzzed by to distract me. No people passed by. I changed focus and began examining the fireplace, the walls, the pictures, the sparse furniture, and all the personal trinkets on display. Suddenly the harsh sound of my name jolted my attention and focus back to Sister sitting on the arm of the chair looming above me like a big fat crow surveying a piece of carrion.

"So, Gabrielle."

"Ahh, yea." I had no idea where she was going. I began braiding the long tassels that hung from my woolen neck scarf.

"What do you think of Tom?"

A trick question. He's her nephew, and I knew I had to say nice things about him.

"He's a fine build of a man," I said, hoping to flatter her.

"Isn't he though? He is very handsome too," she added.

"He is that," I said, making use of one of Mother's learned phrases that make useless conversation sound meaningful.

"You know he has a fine farm and a two story house with slates on top?"

She went on to revisit his merits, those previously discussed at dinner. But she added one more.

"He's very well in with the local parish priest you know."

"Isn't that great," I said.

It seems I was a bit slow in the head and didn't respond correctly to this bit of information, so she was forced to be a bit more explicit.

"Tom and the parish priest are like that," she said excitedly as she held up two fingers stuck together. "And, well, you see," she hesitated before adding, "if you and Tom," she hesitated once more, "were married like," she hesitated again, looking at me wondering if she still needed to spell everything out for me.

She did.

"Sure, the parish priest would give you the next available job in the school. Wouldn't it be grand?"

There was a long pause.

"Well, what do you think of that?" she went on.

Quick wit and sharp brain synapses were not God's gifts to me. I missed roll call when he passed those out. It took a minute for me to process what she had just said. When her intentions finally became clear, I stared at her in disbelief, my jaw hung loose, and a wet glaze blurred my vision. A chill swept over me so fast I began to tremble, making it necessary to bite down on my tongue to prevent my teeth from chattering, which they tend to do in such situations. My mind whirled in confusion. *What am I going to do? She's a nun in my aunt's convent! I can't lose my temper. I can't be rude. I can't agree to this. I have to play along. Sweet God in heaven, help me!"* I begged, as I began to panic. *What am I going to do? How am I going to get out of this?*

There we were: Sister planning my wedding, and I sitting there like a defeated idiot braiding the tassels of my woolen scarf with not a word to say for myself. I could conjure neither a polite nor a rude reaction. My brain had conked out, and my mouth was clenched shut.

"Well, now, I'm thrilled that that's settled," she said, beaming. She clapped her hands and jumped to her feet delighted with herself.

I screamed at my brain. *You can't let her leave the room and make an announcement. You've got to stop her.*

"But I can't get married," I blurted into the discontented silence of the room. "I'm too young."

"Yerra," she coaxed as she sat back down. "Age doesn't matter a whit."

"But I want to live a little. Go out and see the world," I protested.

"Sure Tom wouldn't be opposed to taking you out once in awhile, and you'd have a honeymoon."

I braided some more, struggling to pull another excuse out of the red yarn.

"And," she continued filling the void and getting excited, "I was thinking that you could be engaged tonight and married by Easter. You and your brother could make it a double wedding if you like. Wouldn't that be wonderful?"

"But I couldn't infringe upon his plans," I said stupidly.

"You wouldn't be. Child, every family dreams of a double wedding, and then one wedding makes another, and pretty soon the whole family is married. Lord, sure it is every mother's dream," she went on fantasizing.

Every mother's dream, my eye! I thought. My mother just wants us all out of the house. She couldn't care less if we were married or not. "Just get out of here and don't ever come back," is her cant. To which she often adds, "And never marry a farmer. You'll be a slave your whole life." However, I'm her special case; the slingad of the family, the black soothy thing, with no prospects. She would be willing to break all the rules to get rid of me. Then in terror I remembered another of her cants,: "Better to be an old man's darling than a young man's slave! I'll be a slave and an old man's darling!"

"This is all very sudden," I replied. "I really need to think about this. I can't just decide right here and now."

"Of course you need time," she said. "Let's go back to the kitchen, and we'll have some more tea. Sure you have all the time in the world to think about it. The engagement celebration isn't until seven at the Lakeside Hotel tonight."

Jaisus, I panicked. *An engagement party! Seven o clock tonight! This is a done deal.*

I recalled Mother's warnings that if you broke off an engagement you could be sued for breach of promise. She knew a girl whose reputation was ruined because she was sued for breach of promise. No one would have a thing to do with her thereafter. She had to pack her bags and go to America.

I followed Sister back into the kitchen and headed straight to the fireside chair opposite Carmel. When she saw my tear-flooded eyes, she lost the grin and became serious right away.

"Are you alright?" she asked in French.

Irish was our secret language in foreign lands, while French was our secret language among the uneducated or older generation. We felt safe that no one in the room knew a lick of French.

"We have to get out of here," I stressed.

"I know," she replied.

"No, you don't. You don't understand at all. We have to get out of here right now. Right now!" I repeated.

"We can't just up and leave. We need a ride back to the city. We need them to take us back to the city," she reiterated through clenched teeth.

God spoke to me, or at least someone did, because for the first time all night I was truly inspired.

"I have a plan. I'm going to tell them we have to be back in the city to meet the landlord to let us into the flat."

"What flat?" Carmel asked.

"We can't hitch home. They could follow us. We'll have to stay at Mary Mahoney's flat. I've had a set of keys to her place since college."

"Do you have them with you?"

I rattled a keychain that held my Swiss army knife and a bunch of keys. "Play along with everything I say," I urged.

She burst out laughing.

"This is no laughing matter. You have no idea what sort of predicament we are in. We are in serious trouble," I tried to explain.

She grinned back at me. "I know. I know."

"No you don't," I began angrily as my temper got up. How the hell could she have any idea what was going on here? I had no idea myself until a moment ago. And even then I had to be told to my face.

"Listen, Carmel, this is no laughing matter," I snapped. "We must get out of here now. So be ready to go when I say so."

The sharp-eared nun noticed some distress among us and interrupted, "Is everything all right?"

"Actually, no!" I replied. "We have a bit of a predicament. Carmel just reminded me we needed to be in Limerick city before six to meet the landlord of the flat. He has the keys."

"That's not a problem at all," she rejoiced almost. "If you tell us the address, one of the boys will nip into Limerick and get the keys for you."

"We don't know the address," piped Carmel.

"Yea, we just know how to get there," I continued, thankful for Carmel's smarts.

"Maybe the boys could take us into the city so we could all get the keys," she added.

I glared at her, fit to be tied. What was she up to now? She still thinks this is one big game.

"That's a brilliant idea," Sister agreed. "Boys, drive the girls into the city. Don't be long now. We have plans for seven."

I rushed to put my coat on. Carmel was already walking down the hallway, a great big grin still plastered across her face. She could have been the Jokeress for a new Batman movie the way she carried on. Sister cornered me in the hallway for a few words of encouragement.

"Hurry back now, and don't be long. We have great plans for this evening."

She nodded, winked, and grinned. I wasn't interested in what she had to say. I was focused on a commotion going on behind her. Carmel was having a bit of a scuffle with the house owner over the seating arrangements in the car. By the time I rushed out, she was sitting in the back with the knobs pushed down. She let me in. Tom was hot on my heels and made to get in beside me. I promptly pushed the knob down and pointed toward the front. He had no option but to join his brother in front. Carmel whispered proudly that she had foiled their little seating plan. Well, it didn't really matter, because Tom tugged on the rearview mirror and trained it on my face the whole trip. I played with the keys in my lap while Carmel giggled, laughed, and prodded me. As we neared the flat, I warned Carmel,

"When they stop the car, count to three and we'll jump out at the exact same time."

To be honest I didn't care if Carmel was in or out of the car, but I wanted to be well out before they copped our plan. The car slowed to the curb. Tom was silent, but the brother announced that we should just sit and chat while we waited for the landlord to arrive. I agreed.

"One, two, three!"

We opened the doors in unison and jumped out. I ran down the path like one chased by the devil from hell, fumbled the keys trying to get them into the lock, then burst inside, never once looking back. I collapsed into a sobbing heap just inside the door on the bottom step of the stairs. Carmel hot on my heels, slammed the door shut, drew the bolts, and threw herself onto the couch, laughing like a rabid hyena.

"Oh for goodness sake, Gabrielle," she said later. "How could you be so stupid? They followed all the traditional rules of a match. It couldn't have been more obvious what was going on."

"But I thought there was going to be a very important person coming. I thought it was going to be a priest, and that he would have the giving of a job," I sobbed.

"Tom was the very important person."

"How was I to know?"

"Sometimes, Gabrielle, you're as thick as a board. It was obvious it was a match from the very beginning. We were brought to the home of the head of the family. We were treated to a meal. Your attributes were listed. His attributes were listed. I presume the contract was agreed upon in the room between you and Sister?"

She explained all this like I was a first grader learning how to tie my shoes.

"The whole deal at the hotel tonight was to be the presentation of an engagement ring, trading of whiskey or poteen to seal the deal, and of course setting the date. All that was left was for you to walk the farm the night before the wedding. How dumb can you be? And you're the one into all things Irish?"

"And I'll tell you one more thing," she added, "you're lucky you have a witness for this story. Who'd ever believe you?"

THE FLOWER OF YOUTH

The bishop's house was my first interview, and the nun's nephew my first proposal. While interviews were few and far between, three proposals followed in fairly quick succession. I began to wonder about all those girls who landed on their feet right after college and were now happily married with full-time teaching positions. Obviously I was missing something. Was there a code, a system, a cultural thing that no one ever bothered to tell me about? It wouldn't be the first time no one ever bothered to tell me things. It seems I spent my life playing catch up, trying to figure things out, after the fact, from books. However, back then, in Ireland, there was no after- college-manual. There I was, newly graduated, still unemployed, yet no shortage of potential husbands coming to the door when all I wanted was a job and my freedom.

"Sure, why don't you marry, Paul?" mother said. "He's a lovely lad with a permanent, pensionable, government job. You'd never look back."

"I'm twenty-one and in no hurry to settle," I tried to explain. But Mother didn't understand. Settling me was a priority. Once married I would be someone else's problem!

"You're too fussy, and you're not getting any prettier. If I were you, I'd take what I could get. Maher women don't appreciate with age."

"I don't care."

"Oh, you'll care soon enough when the flower of youth wilts and all you're left with is the convent. Praise be to the Mother of God, your aunt is holding a place for you. At least we have comfort in that."

"Sure, what worry is on you then? I'll be fine. When all else fails, welcome the nunnery," I scoffed insolently.

"You know it all! You're the smart one! There's no talking to you at all," my mother snapped. "Thank God your sister is on her way from America. Maybe she'll talk sense into you."

And sure enough my sister came home from America with her two babies in tow. Gorgeous, lovely babies! However, after a week of baby burping, wiping spit and slobber, changing shitty nappies, and enduring colicky sleepless nights I was cured of any hint of an attraction I may have had toward babies and marriage. Five years my senior, Paul had other ideas. One day he showed up pumped with excitement. His grandmother had given him a site, and now he could build. I was energized too.

The idea of designing and building a house from scratch was exhilarating. Carmel, who seemed to know me better than I knew myself, cornered me one day and quizzed, "Do you plan to marry Paul?"

"Lord no!" said I vehemently.

"Then why are you building a house with him?"

"It'll be a blast. I'd love to design and build a house."

"Did it ever occur to you that he might be thinking that you'll be the little woman in the kitchen of this house? You design the sink because you'll be the one using it!"

"I don't know where he'd have gotten that idea," I said indignantly. "I never agreed to marry him."

"Has he popped the question?"

"Yea, but!!!"

"God, Gabrielle, what kind of a lúdramán are you? What did you tell him?"

"That I was too young to get married, of course."

"Did he say he'd wait for you?"

"Yea, but I'll be long gone before then."

"Poor Paul!" she sighed. "By the way, there's a letter for you. It's a thin one."

Fat letters were refusals, because they returned the curriculum vitae (CV). Thin letters were interview offers, because they kept the CV. A local, rural, country school had a vacancy and invited me to interview. I was skittish with excitement, only to discover the interview was the same day as my sister's children's baptisms. The baptism promised to

be a huge affair, a regular gathering of the clan with the
first grandkids home from America!

"You have to go do that interview," Mother insisted.

"I know."

As luck would have it, the priest called to say he had to move the time because of a previous engagement. Now I could do both. Paul was delighted about the interview and agreed to drive me directly from the baptism to the hotel. On the day of the baptism, everyone showed up to the church in their finest.

"There you are Paul, time you started getting a bit of training," Mother mocked as she shoved the heavily laden nappy bag into Paul's empty hands. I manned the camera. It was a momentous occasion. Three generations baptized in the church my ancestors built. The Maher tradition lived on! The after party was a blast, and I ventured to have a glass of wine, knowing full well that wine either makes me sleepy or a gibbering idiot. On this day of royal excitement I became the idiot.

Three o'clock found me at my interview a little unsteady of foot, ruddy in the face, and extremely loose tongued. It was a three-person panel. From my first glance at him, I didn't like the look of the principal. He was far too polished and smooth for a rural school. He wore expensive tweed, a fancy shirt and tie, and his hair slicked back in a trendy youthful style. The antiquated priest was almost asleep, showing no interest in the proceedings whatsoever, and the fourth-class teacher was all sharp corners with short cropped jet-black hair, a long narrow nose, tight thin lips, and beady black eyes. I knew immediately the job was already given, and they were only going through the motions required by the Teacher's Union. I got my sassy up and let them have it for wasting my time. (And there a good party going on at home!) Needless to say, I didn't get the job. Paul was devastated and promised to do all he could to pull strings in his own parish. Mother was furious and wouldn't talk to me for a week—which I greatly appreciated! Eventually, though, I got the full brunt of her anger.

"God, am I to be stuck looking at you till the end of my days? It's that smart attitude of yours that keeps you from getting a job, and you refuse to get married! You are an embarrassment to the family, you know?"

"Don't worry about it," I said, laughing. "There's always the convent!"

"At this rate of going even they won't have you!"

Months of interviews, and still no luck! The year was getting old, and I had no job. Fortunately there was great demand for substitute teachers, and I was kept busy. Nonetheless, it galled Mother to no end that after all my education I had failed to get a position. She was getting sick of looking at me and complained that my brazen face and attitude didn't help my case any. Sundays were the worst. After mass the women of the parish congregated outside the church gates bragging about their children's successes in marriage, education, or employment.

"And there I was in the middle of the lot of them with nothing to say for myself, because all I have is this useless oschler sitting on her arse at home, one more mouth to feed, and she refuses to lead or drive in an effort to settle herself," Mother complained bitterly.

Every single day the postman threw those dreaded fat envelopes in the door at me. It wasn't long before I simply tossed them unopened into the bottom drawer of the filing cabinet. At some point I ran out of curricula vita and was forced to rummage through the rejection drawer. Carmel and I pulled out the stack of fat envelopes, plopped ourselves down by the fire, and made a huge production of reading the refusals. We put on angry voices, nice voices, sympathetic voices, stern voices, and nasty voices, until it became a competition as to who did the best rendition of a principal rejecting applicants. One by one we threw the letters on the fire and watched them curl up at the edges and slowly burn toward the middle. I imagined them as principals going up in smoke: a slow lingering death with their politically correct rejections. We were pretty near the end of the pile when I began reading a letter that didn't follow the standard rejection. This was a fat envelope with a job offer! My blood ran cold, my collar tightened, my mouth went dry. I read and reread the short letter that offered me a job for a position I had never interviewed for. It was most bizarre. Carmel noticed the absence of my obscenities and looked up. The color had drained from my face, and I was quite pale.

"What's wrong?"

"I'm not sure," I replied, confused.

She snatched the letter from me and began to read.

"This is a job offer!" she exclaimed.

"I know. I can read too! But I never interviewed for that job."

"It's a school in Donegal," she added in surprise. "Well you must have applied there?"

"I apply for every job advertised. Every school in the country has an application on file from me."

I grabbed the letter back and read the address.

"My God, Donegal! That's the end of the world. Don't you remember the bishop's house? It took us a whole day to get there!"

"That was a blast. Do you think the bishop told him about you?"

"Hardly, seeing as you guys ransacked the place."

"Where in Donegal is Stranorlar, anyway?" Carmel queried. In an instant she was gone, returning all excited with a Michelin map.

"This has every village in Ireland on it. If it exists it's here," she said with authority.

We laid the map flat on the kitchen table and used a ruler to comb the county, but we couldn't find a Stranorlar anywhere.

"God, it's not even on the map."

"It must be very small if it's not on the map. Let's call Bill. He'll know where it is," Carmel suggested.

Bill, our neighbor, knew everything about Ireland. He had traveled the length and breadth of the country for work. If he didn't know where it was, he knew people who would. He could even ask the guards for us. It had to be a place somewhere. I began rereading the letter. It was a job offer from a monsignor who was the manager of the school. He wanted me to begin work April 1. That was only two weeks away. The letter was a month old. I was sick to the pit of my stomach. Thoughts stabbed at my mind like quick short bolts of lightning. A job offer in Donegal! Without an interview! Was this some sort of trick to get me back to Donegal so the bishop could get even? Was it an April's Fools joke? Donegal was the last place God made. "England and America are closer than Donegal," I muttered to no one in particular.

I read the letter again. Part of me wanted to pretend that I never got it. If I burned it, no one would ever know. Yes, they would! Carmel would! And she has a mouth as big as a torn slipper. Then the other voice inside me said I needed to get out of this place and get on with my life regardless of where it was. Anything was a start. Besides, if I didn't get a job soon Mother would marry me off to someone while I slept. I recalled the night I had to jump out the upstairs window because there was a potential suitor down stairs waiting for me. He was from a local family of good stock, a second son in line for the outside farm.

"Sure you'll have plenty between the pair of you, with your teaching job and his farm. What more could you want?" she preached.

"And, you know if you marry a farmer," added Uncle Tom, whom she had hauled in to convince me, "you won't be left with only his clothes in the closet if he dies on you."

"You could do a lot worse," Mother interjected.

"Yea, and by the same token, you are always telling us never marry a farmer," I shot back nastily.

"Well these are desperate times, and you're a desperate case. Besides there are seven more mouths to feed after you, madam! It's time you were gone."

How I hated these lectures and the stream of aunts and uncles dragged in to stress the argument. My mind conjured up all the other men waiting downstairs for me, and me only twenty-one and a whole life of cavorting and cajoling ahead of me. Sooner or later I was going to be entrapped, and I knew it. She'd have someone standing below to catch me if I jumped out the window again. I had to go to Donegal. I had to take this job. Carmel rushed in all excited, interrupting my reverie.

"Bill said it was also called Ballybofey. They're twin towns. He's on his way over."

We dashed back to the Michelin map, and there it was, right in the middle of Donegal, a small dot called Ballybofey. I had never heard of that town either. We leaned over the table, the pair of us, staring down at the map. I was judging distances from places I knew and from home. I don't know what Carmel was thinking. In walked Bill.

"So, I hear you're off to Donegal?" he pronounced, like it was a done deal all signed and sealed.

I burst into tears. Bill took one look at me and threw himself into the overstuffed fireside chair. Ignoring my sobbing, he began telling us about my future home.

"Ballybofey and Stranorlar are two tiny towns that straddle the river Finn. One side of the bridge is Ballybofey and the other side is Stranorlar. But it is mostly called Ballybofey because the post office is in Ballybofey."

I was trying desperately to control my sobs and listen to Bill at the same time. His every word was vital. This was my future we were talking about. He went on to say it was a nice enough place, smaller than our town, but the scenery was magnificent and the people friendly. As was characteristic of Bill, by the time he was leaving, we were laughing hysterically about his escapades across the border, which were only a few miles from Stranorlar.

Eventually, yet reluctantly, I told Mother the "good news."

"Ring the priest right away and tell him that you'll accept the job," she insisted.

"I'll ring him tonight. He's probably not home during the day. He's a monsignor and probably very busy," I replied, hoping to postpone the call.

That evening I called the monsignor and was told that the job was still mine, if I wanted it. It was a four-teacher school. I would be teaching first and second class combined. I would need a car. He suggested arriving a few days early to get a feel for the place and to find lodgings. Then he hung up. The conversation was short and sweet. I got off the phone perplexed. I was expected to just show up and get to work and get on with it.

"Sure, what did you expect?" Mother snapped.

"I dunno," I mused.

"Well, we have just one week to find you a car," she said. "I hope you've saved your sub money!"

It was a whirlwind week. I had a job offer. The bank gave me a loan. I bought a car. I was moving to Donegal; the last outpost before the Arctic! But this time, I had a job to go to!

OUT THE GAP

For a whole week the map of Ireland laid spread across the dining room table. Everyone who came or left the house during that time was asked their opinion on the fastest route to Donegal without going through the North, which was a hot bed of terrorist activities in the early eighties. Most people agreed on the route through Athlone, Roscommon, and Sligo, skirting the North at Ballyshannon and on up to Donegal town. They bowed their heads and made condolences with me as they left the house. Everyone, absolutely everyone, no exceptions, seemed to be of the same opinion: I was going away—far, far, away—and they felt deeply sorry for me. It was a long week of waking the dead. I was the bereaved and the deceased, the receiving end of handshakes, tears, shaking heads, and much sympathy. When all was quiet, I grabbed a fat red marker and circled the towns that formed the stepping stones of my journey north. Mother was delirious with excitement. Gabrielle finally had a job, a permanent, pensionable government job! Every mother's dream!

"Lord, isn't it great? It's the answer to all my prayers," she declared excitedly to Uncle Tom one night. "Now all she needs is a husband, and then she's off my hands and someone else's problem. May God help whomever takes her!"

"Oh, the stag is in her," agreed Uncle Tom. "She won't go easy."

That morning I walked to my Mazda 323, which was loaded to the ceiling with winter clothes for the brutal Arctic conditions I expected in Donegal. My stomach was a heavy ball of undigested food, my heart shattered, my ego bruised, and my body limp at the prospects of this trip into the abyss of oblivion. My mother pushed me out the door like she was delighted to be rid of me, and Daddy was his usual narcissistic self, more interested in promoting his home-brew wine than mourning the loss of his daughter. I felt unloved and unwanted. It was with such sentiments I left home. Only Carmel shared my grief, all be it she was mourning the loss of her freedom and good times. She was distraught at the thought of losing me. I was her only peer in the house, and life would be cold and empty with no big sister to bother, nag, or keep on track. Her fun and games were about to end.

When I went to say goodbye to Daddy he was busy stirring huge vats of fermenting wine. His circular response was as expected.

"Daddy, I'm off to Donegal now. I'll see you when I see you, I suppose."

"Sure, isn't that grand! Would you like to take a few bottles with you?" he offered of his latest batch of elderberry wine.

"Daddy, I don't drink it, and I don't know anyone there. What would I do with it?"

"True, true, true," was his lame reply.

"Well, Daddy, I'm off. I don't know when I'll be home again. It's hours away."

"Sure, we'll see you when we see you."

Mother prepared the usual breakfast, brown-bread toast and tea. We sat at the dining room table making small talk.

"Have you everything packed?"

"Yep, I did it all last night. The car is packed to the gills."

"Grand, grand, and the tires are pumped?"

"Yep, I filled up with petrol last night as well."

"What about the water in the radiator?"

"Yea, I checked that too. It's fine."

Eventually, it was time to go. Mother grabbed the plastic Holy Mary bottle from the top of the fridge and walked behind me to the door. I climbed into the car and rolled down the window.

"Off you go now," Mother said. 'Tis for the best. Every bird leaves the nest. It's nature. Don't forget to say your prayers and go to Mass."

"I won't," my eyes filled with tears. I didn't want to cry in front of Mother. She noticed my distress and comforted me.

"You're out the gap now, Gabrielle. You have a job and a place to go. It's time to make a life for yourself. There's nothing here for you."

She unscrewed the bottle, poured the blessed Lourdes water into the palm of her hand, and threw it at me. We blessed ourselves in unison. Grudgingly, I started the engine and slowly reversed through the gates, where I swung the car around, paused one last time before driving the length of the driveway toward the main road. Mother stood in the open door way waving me off until I was out of sight.

Carmel stayed home from school that morning with plans for me to drop her off at the school gate on my route to Donegal. She would be late, but didn't care. She was angry at me, at Mother, at Dad, at my situation, at the whole world. All the way into town she ranted and raved about the injustice of it. I pulled the car parallel with the school gate and waited for her to get out. When she did, she took one look back at me before bursting into tears. Her English teacher was returning from lunch and saluted her warmly. She spat him a nasty reply. On recognizing her distressed state, he timidly approached my car. I explained the situation, shouting at him through the open door. He smiled kindly at me, shut the car door, and gently took Carmel by the elbow. I watched him escort her limp, rhythmically heaving body through the school gates. Then I revved up the engine and drove toward Roscrea, the first red stepping-stone toward my lonely exile.

Roscrea to Birr was familiar territory, so I cruised on autopilot. However, outside Birr I needed to consult my map. From this point forward all was new terrain and appeared to be a series of convoluted turns and twists and lefts and rights the whole way to Donegal. When I left the main road outside Birr, brown powdery earth stretched out before me all the way to the horizon. I burst into tears and sobbed at my pitiful situation. My overactive imagination was going wild with ridiculous scenarios. I was reminded of the deserts of Africa all yellow instead of brown. Either which way, bog or desert, this was my destiny, a cast out, with no one to accompany me, no one to love me, no one to care about me, all alone in the great wide world to wander aimlessly for the rest of my days like the Israelites wandering for forty years around the Sinai Peninsula. I thought of Mary begging for a room at the inn. I too had no idea where I was to lay my head that night.

I genuinely believed I would never go home again and that no one could care less. I was gone, forgotten, one less burden, another county's problem now. By the time I had driven through the bog, I had cried myself dry. I had cursed the people of my past, the Irish government, the teacher's union, teaching in general, the system, and just about everything and everyone I had ever known. Tears and sadness were banished and soon replaced by a ferocious anger triggered by the crossing of the Bridge of Athlone.

My mind recalled those brave men running out one by one to chop down the wooden bridge while under fire from the enemy. Each and every one of

them was willing to die for their beloved Ireland—
and for freedom. In 1690 the Williamite Army
(fighting for William of Orange) controlled most of
the land east of the Shannon River. They marched
westward toward Athlone with plans to cross the
River Shannon and take the west. Jacobite forces
(fighting for James II of England) battled hard to
prevent the Williamites from crossing the river. As I
drove, a poem came to my mind, a poem that
describes the bravery of the men under Sergeant
Custume. They managed to dislodge the bridge of
Athlone in shifts. The felling of the bridge slowed
the westward progress of the Williamites.
Unfortunately they forded the river farther south.

The Bridge of Athlone
by Aubrey De Vere (1814-1902)

Does any man that a Gael can fear?
Of a thousand deeds let him learn but one!
The Shannon swept onward, broad and clear,
Between the leaguers and broad Athlone.
"Break down that bridge."
Six warriors rushed
Through the storm of shot and the storm of
shell.
With late but certain victory flushed,
The grim Dutch gunners eyed them well.
They fell in death, their work half done:
They wrenched at the planks "mid a hail of
fire."
The bridge stood fast; and nigh and nigher.

The foe swarmed darkly, densely on.
Oh, who for Erin will strike a stroke?
Who hurl yon planks where the waters roar?
Six warriors forth from their commanders broke,
And flung them upon that bridge once more.
Again at the rocking planks they dashed,
And four dropped dead; and two remained.
The huge beams groaned and the arch down crashed.
Two stalwart swimmers the margin gained.

(Flowers from Many Gardens: A New Anthology by a Christian Brother, M. H. Gill and Son, LTD. Dublin, 56.)

My nationalistic sentiments were heightened. I hated the British for what my people suffered under their seven- hundred-year rule. This was hardly the mindset to cultivate as I headed North toward the border!

Outside Roscommon I passed a crossroads village where an elderly friend of mine was born. She had told me once, "Gabrielle, great things await you. You are destined to go far."

Yea right! I thought. *Banishment to Donegal is hardly what she had in mind.* With such reminiscences, outburst, tears, and tantrums, I arrived in Donegal town. *Not long more*, I thought. *Just one more town and I'm there.*

Leaving Donegal town for the last leg of my trip, I felt relieved that I had made it this far without incident—no puncture, no accident; I didn't even get lost. A few miles on the far side of Donegal town, the scenery took a turn for the worse. Nothing could have prepared me for the last step of the trip. I had been to the Gap of Dunloe, Moll's Gap, Bearnán Éile, and many other gaps in my day, but Barnesmore Gap is the daddy of all gaps. *Barnesmore* literally translated means "the big gap." It is probably the largest gap in all of Ireland. It might even be the largest gap in the world!

Two tall mountain ranges gouged by glacial erosion rise out of the ground like the massive shoulders of combatant giants. The road snakes between these looming, barren forms, which cast great shadows of despair across the road, forcing me to drive right through them. On my left, the mountain dropped straight down, forming a jagged road edge. Little waterfalls sprung from the surface at precarious angles and splashed into gullies before disappearing into invisible streams or swallow holes. The other side of the road, an ice-carved valley, scooped to meet me. My geography lessons flooded back, and I enjoyed picking out various landforms, most notably the ribbon lakes that stretched out before me for miles. A handful of white sheep scuttled about on the desolate slopes. Stranorlar was at the opposite end of a time warp, a brown hole, separating it from all known civilization—and separating me from all I knew and loved. Tears sprung forth, imitating the little waterfalls on the roadside. I cried and cried as I drove through that gap thinking there was no end in sight, ever. I composed a ditty to confirm my desolate state.

I left home to go
Around the woods, (home)
Into the bog, (Ferbane)
Across the river, (Shannon)
Over the mountain, (Curlews)
Along the coast, (Sligo)
And through the gap, (Barnesmore)
To my new abode,
Where I am to be alone,
Unknown,
Unloved.
Yet, I dared
To take this road.

I found myself at the edge of a two-mile-long town that seemed stretched evenly on either side of a centerpiece bridge spanning the River Finn. I had no idea what to do now that I had gotten here, so I drove to the end of town, turned around, came back, and decided to pay a visit to the church in hope of some inspiration. God spoke!

"Go knock on the priest's door," he said.

Brilliant idea! I thought. So I did. I found his cottage almost hidden behind the church.

A large roly-poly man stretched into a black suit and white collar answered the door. His lips and teeth were sprinkled with breadcrumbs tastefully highlighted by the odd raspberry seed. He was obviously annoyed at having being disturbed during his supper and gaped at me, smacking his lips and sucking through the wind holes between his teeth. My feet turned to jelly, my stomach began to growl, and my brain froze like it tends to when put on the spot. No clever ditties or cheerful greeting sprang to mind. No, just the usual stupid stuff like, "Am, is this the Parochial House?"

Yah, eejit, I responded internally to my own question. *Of course it its! Where else do you think it is? Besides the big brass sign says it right here.*

"Is there something I can do for you?" the priest responded through lose blubbery old man's lips.

"I'm Gabrielle Maher," I began

He looked at me dumbly like I had said nothing at all. So I continued, "The St. Anthony's job? The new teacher?"

"Oh, yes," he replied, and the conversation stopped right there, as if every word cost him money.

I stood looking at him, and he at me, both vacant species eyeing each other. An empty silence hung on the air as I struggled to find my intellectual and verbal ability.

"I need a place to stay for the night. I just got here and I don't know anyone," I blurted. Almost instantly he disappeared into the darkness, leaving me standing at the open door wondering if he was ever coming back. He returned holding a torn slip of paper with an address scribbled on it.

"There, that's the name and address of a good B&B. Down the road, to the left, you can't miss it. There's a sign out front." He swallowed hard and stated rather than asked, "You'll be at the school tomorrow!"

"I don't know where the school is," I replied sheepishly.

"Out the Fintown road, you can't miss it," he muttered as he turned and shut the door.

Great, said I to myself in shock. *So this is Donegal, and he's my manager!*

I surveyed the parking lot behind the cottage and noticed that this was indeed a large church attached to the town school. So I was to be teaching in the country school. I stood there for a while, shoving that moving introduction into some remote corner of my brain. Then I climbed back into the car and with great difficulty found the B&B.

The woman of the house was delightful. She gave me explicit directions to the school and assured me that it was a great school with a lovely principal. She went on to say it had a very high standard of Irish and the parents and children were from the finest families. She insisted I would be much happier teaching out there than in the town school. This set me at ease.

On the morrow, I got up extra early to be sure to arrive in plenty of time. The car failed to start. The battery was dead. I had left the lights on all night. By the time the landlady had arranged help, I was an hour late for my first day at work. The principal assured me it could happen to a bishop, while the teacher standing at his right curled up her nose and scowled like I was an infection in her airspace. I knew then and there I had won some, and I had lost some.

There is no denying the rest of the staff welcomed me in turn and were sincere in their warmth toward me. The B&B lady had been right. Many parents came to meet and greet "the girl from the south" after school. They too were congenial and excited at the prospects of "such a pretty young thing" teaching their children.

I settled into my new school, my new job, and in no time made new friends. As the youngest on staff, the older teachers delighted in coaching me, advising me, and living vicariously through my escapades. I made every mistake possible with regard to the delicate English/Irish cross-border situation.

"When are you going to heed my advice about crossing the border?" Mrs. Allgood exclaimed every Monday morning. "A young girl like you has no business over there. You have no idea what trouble you could get into," she went on.

And stupid, stupid me never listened.

WRONG ATTITUDE

Our neighbors on both sides were Protestant. We were friends and never thought about each other in terms of opposite sides, different religions, or anything other than good neighbors. We went to their birthday parties, wakes, and weddings. We invited them to ours. We even went to funerals in the Protestant church, the only caution being not to receive communion because we weren't Protestant. That made perfect sense. If you're not a member, you don't get the full benefits. Membership rules applied everywhere: the racquetball club, the youth club, the golf club, the Garda Swimming Pool, even the private schools. It was nothing to us that they were Protestant. It didn't occur to us to think any differently. However, in the north there were places where you were defined by your religion. I also discovered that you were equally defined by your name and nationality. Sometimes I had the wrong name, which in turn implied the wrong religion, and the wrong nationality. The North was indeed a bizarre place, and I was obsessed with it.

My fixation began with that initial trip across the border from Donegal to Strabane. I drove to the first border crossing I met and turned into a very narrow road leading across the River Finn through two check points. The first check point was the Irish Gardaí, allowing me to exit the Free State. The second check point was the British, allowing me to enter their claimed state of Northern Ireland. The Garda check point was little more than a one-room shack leaning toward the river. One Garda sat inside sipping on a cup of tea and pulling on a cigarette, while the other leaned on the jar of the door talking in at him. He turned his head to look at the oncoming car, and not bothering to budge, he waved me on.

That was easy, I thought. *I don't know what all the fuss is about.*

Having crossed the narrow bridge spanning the political border, a sharp turn in the road brought me level with a ramp. I slammed on my brakes and eased over it. Immediately ahead of me was another road ramp beyond which loomed a tall, gray, wooden military fort edged and trimmed with barbed wire. Policemen scurried to and fro like cockroaches. They were armed to the teeth with hip guns, rifles, bulletproof vests, and an assortment of other belt equipment. I stopped between the two road ramps, which I later discovered were called humps. Two policemen in greenish black uniforms beckoned me toward them.

No, way, I thought.

I looked around to see if I could reverse and go back, but the road was too narrow. I noticed it was deliberately reverse-funnel shaped, forcing one toward the blockade and preventing escape. A brilliant design! I was trapped. They waved to me again. I eased the car forward until my bumper was level with the barrier. Then I sat there and began chiding myself for not taking people's advice. Here I was, alone in the middle of nowhere, surrounded by dozens of armed soldiers and equally laden policemen.

No one will ever miss me.

Someone tapped on the window. I rolled it down. A soldier holding a rifle angled toward me, bent low to the open window, and politely asked, "Can I see your license, please?"

I handed it to him.

"What kind of a name is that?" he asked.

"It's Irish," I responded, proud as can be of my Irish-spelled name complete with fadas and seimhús. Years previously, while a diligent student of Irish, I had reverted to using my Irish name, Ní Mheachair, instead of Maher. I proudly refused to bear an English tag.

"Irish! Southern!" he retorted.

"What's wrong with that?" I sassed back.

"We don't get many Southern-registered cars around here, not at this crossing. What are you doing all the way up here?"

"I live in Ballybofey now."

"Hmmm."

He shoved the license back at me and continued, "Would you mind getting out of the car and opening the boot for us?"

"Here's the key; you can do it yourself."

"Sorry, miss! Can't do that; it's against policy."

"That's ridiculous!"

"Miss, you could have it booby-trapped."

"Really, like I'm twenty-one years old and going to blow myself up just to get you? Don't be ridiculous!"

"I'm sorry, miss, but its standard procedure, and I'm being monitored," he almost apologized.

"Fine so," I snapped.

As commanded, I unlocked and opened the boot for inspection. Next, I was ordered to open the bonnet.

"See, no bombs! Clean as a whistle!" I mocked.

"Miss, you do know that this is an unofficial border crossing?"

"No, as a matter of fact I don't."

"You're supposed to use the official crossings."

"This is the only crossing I saw on my way here."

"If you had continued a few miles down the road, you would have come to the Camel's Hump. That's the official crossing on this side," he explained.

"Ahhhh! Well, I'll be sure to take that one the next time."

I got back into the car, checked to see if my purse and things were untouched, and waited for the barrier to rise. Then I drove off. As I left the center of that fortress, I noticed I had attracted a large military audience. It made me nervous, yet angry.

"Why do I have to be subjected to such treatment in my own country?" I fumed aloud and decided then and there that I was not letting them or anyone else prevent me from enjoying my own country, North or South. With such a mentality, I found myself looking for trouble in all the wrong places.

The following Monday I told Mrs. Allgood about my exploits on the border. She was livid.

"You stupid, stupid, girl. Don't you know they can plant things on your car and arrest you for it? Rule number one: You never go alone into the North. And rule number two: You never, never, ever let them check your car without following them around, in, and under the car."

"I'll be smarter next time," I muttered.

"Next time?! Is there no talking to you at all?" she exclaimed in disbelief.

"They have no right. It's my country."

"That attitude is going to get you in a lot of trouble, young lady."

And she was right. It did.

The next week I made sure to use the official border crossing at Strabane. I figured they had to be nicer there, since it was an official crossing and I was not breaking any laws or trying to sneak into the North unofficially!

The Strabane border crossing, like the one at Claddy, straddles the river Finn. It is locally known as the Camel's Hump. The name refers to the humpbacked bridge linking Northern Ireland with Southern Ireland or the Free State as the south was referred to up there. On the very crest of this bridge there is an unusually wide road ramp, which makes the angle precariously steep. I was told this ingenious piece of engineering was invented by the British to automatically explode a mercury trigger bomb. Complex chemistry is way beyond my comprehension level, but according to local lore, tipping the car at unstable angles causes the mercury to move, thus triggering the bomb, ensuring it would explode before it reached the military fort. Needless to say, in my time I never heard of a bomb exploding on the border, so it must have been effective in preventing such attacks.

Being the world's worst driver, I had great difficulty getting my little car up and over the hump. There was a long line of traffic, and I had to hold my car on the hump with the handbrake to prevent rolling back into the guy behind me, or lurching forward into the guy ahead of me. By the time the guardrail was in sight I was mentally exhausted. Four fully armed policemen approached my car. Two stood behind the car, and the other two took up position on either side of the front windows. The guy on my side tapped on the window. I rolled it down and handed him my license. He took one look at the cover and didn't even bother to open it. Yet, he made no attempt to return it either. My nerves began to tingle.

"Pull forward, please," he ordered as he pointed to a side lane out of the flow of traffic.

I didn't move. I wanted my license back. He spotted my reluctance and continued.

"Pull forward to the yellow line and wait for further instructions," he went on.

"My license, please. I want it back."

He ignored me.

I pulled the car forward to the yellow line. Almost immediately a police lady came toward me and signaled for me to get out of the car. I got out and smartly made my way to the back of the car with plans to open the boot, just like I had been ordered to do the week before. I was about to put the key in the lock when I found myself surrounded with rifle barrels and a rhythmical clicking noise familiar from the movies. I froze.

Actually, my heart stopped.

"Hand me the keys. Slowly, very slowly," the policewoman ordered as she hesitantly reached toward me like I was a vicious, rabid dog. I carefully passed them toward her, dangling them from the pen knife keychain. The gun barrels were lowered instantly. The policemen slowly withdrew and settled back into the shadows. By now I had slightly wet myself, and the tears were burning at the back of my eyes.

The police lady ushered me into a cavernous cement chamber. The powdery gray walls were bare. The only furniture was a desk with a computer on top, a chair shoved underneath, and a set of three gray plastic chairs lining the opposite wall. I just stood there like a broken robot not knowing which way to turn or look. It seems in the North there is a color-coded stripe for every occasion. "Face the line on the wall. Stand on the white stripe. Pull your vehicle to the yellow stripe." Gently she eased me this way and that until I ended up where she wanted me to be, on the white stripe facing the computer desk. Then she proceeded to frisk me from head to toe. I was terrified she was going to strip-search me. That would have been the ultimate invasion of my territory. But no, the female police officer was professionally polite and did everything in her power to keep me calm. When she confirmed I was not carrying a weapon, she offered me a chair and began to interrogate me. All my answers were entered into the computer. While sitting there I noticed my car being rolled into a larger cement room separated from me by reinforced glass windows. A squad of soldiers garbed in heavily padded clothing attacked it like hungry ants. They went all over it, inside and outside. After what seemed like ages, the ants withdrew, and only one remained partially hidden under the engine of my car. I recalled Mrs. Allgood's warning: "They could plant anything on your car." As I contemplated these cautionary words and became frustrated by my inability to do anything about it, the lady officer turned my attention back to the soldier under my car who was waving an oily gray rag, trying to get our attention.

"Miss," he called to me. "You have an oil leak. Do you mind if I tighten the washer for you?"

"Sure," I replied, quite taken aback.

"Why don't you come out here and let me show you the problem," he suggested. I looked at my lady officer for permission to move. Smiling, she nodded her head in his direction, officially discharging me. He showed me the loose washer, tightened it, and proceeded to dip my oil, water, and window-washer liquid. He even made suggestions on how to maintain my lubrications. Although too nervous to concentrate on the lesson, I appreciated his kindness. When he was done, another officer returned my license and keys declaring I was free to go. I couldn't get out of the concrete prison fast enough. I really wanted to turn around and go home, but the lanes were configured in such a way I could only move forward.

At the Woolworth's parking lot, my emotions let loose. Hot, unwelcome tears spilled down my face. I let them fall. After what seemed like hours, I decided to find a café where I gorged myself on creamy chocolate buns, washing them down with a pot of steaming tea. Fortified with sugar and caffeine, I drove home via Claddy, the unofficial border crossing. The Camel Hump experience had been enough humiliation for one day.

When I eventually shared my story with Mildred, she assured me my ordeal was standard procedure for first-timers crossing at an official point. Once my information was in their computers, there would be no further hassle, unless of course I explicitly went looking for it. Having thus reassured, I returned to crossing the border on a weekly basis with the sincere purpose of enjoying the state-of-the-art sports complex where I exercised, swam, played badminton, tennis, and racquet ball, and for my weekly grocery shopping and petrol fill up. However, nothing about the North was ever simple. Every trip offered a new lesson on life or another grand adventure.

NEW TIRES

After several cross-border escapades, I became familiar with the routine, but the players were puzzling. There were so many different types of military, legal and illegal, it was hard to keep them straight. The authorized military were the Royal Ulster Constabulary (the cops); the Ulster Defense Regiment (Northern Ireland's Army), who recruited from local Northern Irish; and an array of British soldiers. The English wore different colored berets and had harsh English accents. Then there were lists and lists of illegal organizations who fought for a united Ireland or against a united Ireland or favored Catholics or favored Protestants. These organizations used acronyms like LDF, UFF, UVF, UDA, IRA, RIRA, INLA, CIRA, and many, many more. It was almost impossible to figure out what side each was on. I was challenged to keep up with the color codes, abbreviations, and legal status.

The unofficial border at Claddy was my preferred crossing. It was closer to home, the Gardaí waved me on without incident, and I had little trouble at the Northern side, except when there was a change of guard. One day, having successfully passed all the checkpoints, I noticed my car pulling to one side. I was only walking distance from the sports complex.

A flat, just my luck! I thought. To my left I spotted a news agency with petrol pumps. Someone would surely help me change the tire. I explained my predicament to the shopkeeper/owner, and he volunteered to take care of my car while I went off to play my badminton game. He was so nice I couldn't believe my luck and gladly turned my car and keys over to his care.

"How long do you think you'll be gone?"

"The game usually lasts an hour, and then I have a swim. I'll be done in a little under two hours."

"Grand so. I'll have it ready for you by then."

Off I strutted to the sports complex with nothing on my mind other than the game. Two hours later I returned to the news agency. The shopkeeper had my car parked to one side. I checked the tire and found it was mended and ready to go. All I had to do was collect the keys and pay him.

"I'm right sorry about your tire," he confessed.

"What do you mean?"

"That wasn't meant for you, you know."

I was utterly confused by the comment, and it must have been written all over my face. He reached under the counter and pulled out the rubber heel of a man's shoe with four six inch nails piercing through.

"This is what punctured your tire," he explained.

Making no response and staring blankly at the spiked heel, he decided to continue the lesson.

"You see this was meant for an armed patrol, not you. The young lads throw them out on the road to puncture the patrol vehicles," he confessed. "You were unlucky and got caught on one."

"How can I thank you? How much do I owe you?" was my best response.

"Och girl, away with you. I was happy to help."

He gestured me out the door with the flick of his hand   still holding the nail spiked heel.

"Thank you so much," I replied.

What a lovely man! I thought to myself as I drove off. I should have asked him for the heel. It would serve as a trophy piece..

On my way home I had to drop some groceries off with a friend. She wasn't home, but her husband, Josh, was. I told him my story over tea. His face reddened with anger.

"For God's sake, Gabrielle, do you realize what you just did?"

I was afraid to answer him. I had no idea what I had said to trigger such anger.

"You're damn stupid! That man could have been anyone. He could have planted a device on your car in the hour and a half you were gone. Then crossing the border you would have gone up in smoke. Puff!" He snapped his fingers. "Just like that, and no one would have been any the wiser."

The reality of his statement dawned on me. I reddened with embarrassment. To diffuse the volatile atmosphere between us he added kindly, "By the way, I noticed you could do with a new set of tires. I'll give you the address of a man who'll see you right. Unfortunately, his shop is in the North. Do you want me to go with you?"

"That's really kind of you, Josh, but I'll be fine if you give me the address and the directions. Besides, I can't buy anything until my next paycheck."

Everything from Easter eggs to petrol was cheaper in the North. Hence it was no surprise that the best deal on tires was also in the North.

I followed Josh O Neill's directions to the letter. There was nothing but a burned-out site where the tire shop should have been. I continued driving out the same road into the countryside hoping something would turn up. Indeed it did. Jutting awkwardly out of the ditch was a hand-drawn sign, "O Dwyer's Tires," with an arrow pointing into the field behind it. A roughly hewn gap led into the field where I spotted a rusty galvanized hay barn in the far corner of the field.

This is hardly the place, I contemplated.

I drove through the opening in the ditch and followed the newly graveled roadway straight to the doors of the barn. I parked right between the doors and marched inside to find the place lined from floor to ceiling with tires, both old and new.

"Gone! You're right there. It's gone! We were given an hour to get out, so we took what we wanted and scrambled. When we got back, it was gone. Blown away on a breeze, you might say," the guy laughed as he bent over the tire he was mending.

"But that's not funny. It was your business. Aren't you angry?"

"Angry, not at all. It was the best thing they ever did for me."

"Are you one of them?" I dared to ask.

"Yerra, not at all. You're from the South aren't you, wee girl?" he mocked.

"Yea."

"Och, girl, we have it all figured out up here."

I begged for enlightenment.

"Sure the Queen has loads of money. She's going to build me a bigger, better tire shop. And she has to pay for this shed in the meantime. When I'm back in business, I'll have a state-of-the-art place, you wait and see."

A small crowd of workers gathered around, listening and laughing at the silly little Southern girl chatting up the boss. They nodded in agreement as he endeavored to explain the strategy. They too were looking forward to better working conditions, a-la-Queen.

"Didn't you pay for protection?" I went on.

"Protection, of course I paid for protection. Everyone does. But I needed a new place. So my protection will get me the new place. You should have seen the old place. A wreck. Damp, drafty, bad electrics, no toilet facilities; even this is a palace compared."

The lads guffawed, and this time I joined with them. They gave me four new tires for a great price. The lads put them on for me and cheered loudly as I drove out the door. I waved good-bye and was thankful for the lesson. I couldn't wait to tell Mildred. This would beat any story of hers.

384 EHI

Having secured accommodations in a town house with two other girls, I was finally making friends and settling in. Susan and Eileen were lovely girls, and we got along famously. Eileen was from the west of Ireland and worked for the civil service, which had a huge office in Ballybofey. She got a promotion at work and wanted to celebrate her success. Someone suggested the Manor Arms in Castlederg. However, that was across the border, and good girls like Eileen didn't court danger. I volunteered to drive.

Saturday afternoon we drove from Castlefinn across the border and into Castlederg. Eileen was excited about a four-course meal in the hotel and was already raving about what she might order.

"Do you think they'll have salmon?"

"Of course they will."

"Maybe I'll go for a big steak and red wine instead."

"That's what I'm getting with mashed potatoes. I usually get the salmon when Catherine's paying," I joked.

Susan wasn't making any decisions until she saw the menu, but she was definitely having prawn cocktail for a starter.

"Salmon is the only fish I like," I added.

"I'll eat anything if it's fancy," retorted Eileen.

Saturday is the busiest day of the week in most rural towns so parking spots are few and far between. Eventually, I found one on a side street off Main. Then we trotted down the road, to the left, then right, and in the front door of the Manor Arms Hotel. Since Susan had made advance reservations, we were ushered directly to our corner table and immediately handed menus. Eileen was beside herself with excitement, bouncing up and down in her seat like a four-year-old at a birthday party. Obviously she rarely frequented hotels for meals, unlike Susan who came from wealthy parents and I, who actually worked for a hotel during my summer holidays. I got the steak, Eileen the salmon, and Susan the trout. The girls got a bottle of white wine between them. Thankfully, I couldn't drink because I was the chauffeur. They emptied that bottle like they were dying of thirst and ended up all giggly and stupid.

While we ate dinner we could hear sirens going off in the city center. No one in the hotel was bothered, so we weren't either. A police vehicle with a loudspeaker circumnavigated the square several times, making a muffled unintelligible announcement. Everyone ignored that too. After about two hours of eating, giggling, laughing, and storytelling we decided to leave. I would have liked to spend some time shopping in this new town, but with full bellies and spinning heads, neither of them was interested.

"Let's go home. That was so much fun," laughed Eileen.

"Good idea," agreed Susan. "I still have some case work to finish up."

"So no one wants to go shopping?"

"Nope!" snapped Eileen.

"Me neither," added Susan.

"OK then! We're for home so?" I lamented loudly.

We stumbled down Main Street to the side road where I had parked, only to be halted in our tracks by a pair of policemen guarding the entrance. I thought they were stopping us because it was pretty obvious the girls were plastered. But on further inspection we found the whole area was cordoned off with barricades, tape, cones, armored cars, and trucks. Military commotion and the buzz of walkie-talkies dominated the space.

"Ladies, you can't go down that street."

"Why not?"

"It's cornered off by the bomb squad."

"What do you mean it's cornered off by the bomb squad?"

"Miss, there's a car down there parked in a control zone with a bomb in it."

"Oh, my God," shrieked Eileen, "A real live bomb!"

"Yes, miss. Now if you don't mind, you'll have to take an alternate route home."

"But," I started.

He cut me short. "The robot is on its way. You'll have to move on."

"What robot?"

"The robot to detonate the bomb."

"But we can't move on. My car is parked down there!"

"I'm sorry miss, but you'll have to wait until the bomb is detonated and the debris cleared away. Is there somewhere you can go for an hour or so?"

"But what about my car?"

"I'm sorry miss. You'll simply have to wait."

A superior officer saw the commotion and came toward us.

"My car is down that street," I snapped at him, "and he won't let me get it."

"I'm sorry miss but we cannot put you in danger. Which one is your car anyway?"

"It's a beige Mazda 323. It's right there on the right behind the red one." I pointed toward the car surrounded by cones and yellow tape.

"What's your license plate number?"

"I dunno."

"Is it 384 EHI."

"That sounds familiar."

He picked up his walkie-talkie and called to someone down the street who was standing opposite my car a safe enough distance from the impending robot-controlled explosion. This officer pointed to my car and nodded back to the other one.

"Yes, that's my car."

"Miss, do you realize you parked illegally in a control zone?"

"What's a control zone?"

He informed me that single yellow stripes along the pavement meant you could only park there if you left a human being in the car behind you. That way they knew it wasn't primed with a bomb.

"Miss, are you aware that there is a two-hundred-pound fine for illegally parking in a control zone?" he continued.

I about panicked. I don't have two hundred pounds sterling to spare. I could see myself behind bars and people screaming at me for being so stupid.

Oh, dear God, what am I to do?

"Officer, I'm from the South. I had no idea there were different rules about parking up here! I'm really sorry. I'll never do it again."

"Well, miss, we sent a car around town announcing your registration number and asking you to return to your car. Didn't you hear that?"

"I didn't know my license plate number, so I didn't know it was me," I confessed lamely.

"The whole bomb squad, complete with robot, has been called out, and they're on their way. This is most awkward. Most awkward!" he repeated.

I just stood there like an eejit waiting for my sentence. He towered over me, making more calls on his walkie-talkie. Soon I noticed the police removing the tape and cones from around my car and the barricades from both ends of the street. Police, soldiers, and armored cars roared off, disappearing into the city center. Peace was restored. I sneaked a look at the officer. He caught me.

"You're free to go now," he ordered sternly.

I turned to find Susan and Eileen standing one side wide-eyed and scared. I was furiously angry with them. They were no help at all. Couldn't they have flirted or done something to plead my case? At the very least they could have stood beside me for moral support. Instead they played panicked, dumb drunks and had the audacity to complain the whole way home.

"We could have been arrested!" they whined.

Yea, right! Now I knew who my friends were!

AN PHOBLACHT

Mildred was from Cork, the Deep South as we called it. Because she failed to secure a job closer to home, she too was doomed to the Donegal experience. I actually felt sorry for the poor thing. Her fate was worse than mine. She lived at literally the last post of civilization before the Arctic. Carndonagh, the largest town on the Inis Eoghain peninsula, is a few miles south of Malin Head, the most northerly point in Ireland. At least I was an hour south. The pair of us commiserated on a monthly basis when we took turns visiting each other. However, I feel certain I much preferred going to visit her than she did coming to see me. Whenever we got together, we compared Northern Ireland experiences. Mildred was smart, pretty, funny, witty, wise, athletic, and talented in all things. I should have envied her, but she was a sister to me, and I loved everything about her. Besides, she was a saint tolerating the trouble I agitated among her friends and yet she welcomed me back month after month.

The peninsula of Inis Eoghain is one of the most beautiful locations in Ireland. It has forests, beaches, mountains, valleys, lakes, islands, bogs, nightlife, and men. I loved all of those things in no particular order. But the selection of men was staggering compared to the pickings where I was exiled. Carndonagh had an array of men who rivaled the dessert bar on a cruise ship. There were endless delectable choices: fine-bodied athletes who played hurling, rugby, or soccer; buff young farmers; bronzed fishermen; clean-cut bankers; and romantic musicians. I couldn't get enough of the place or the men!

On my very first night out in Carndonagh, we began our pub crawl in a large lounge off the diamond where a folk group played diddly-aye music. A gang of us sat around a table in a secluded alcove. We were an equal mix of guys and girls. Most of us were teachers banished from our homelands, others were simply misfits, outcasts, exiles, or jilted lovers. Such characters make the best company, and on some level I could identify with each and every one of them.

About an hour into our relaxing setting, a tall, bearded giant sauntered into the pub with a heavily laden satchel slung over his shoulder. First he went from person to person along the bar selling his newspapers. Then he began on the secluded alcoves. All the while he never uttered a single word. When he parked himself at the head of our table, everyone quit talking and nervously lowered their eyes toward their drinks. Disregarding their obvious efforts to ignore him, he held his ground and remained silently statuesque. I was utterly confused. Why was this disheveled man looming threateningly over us? Why didn't he talk? Why didn't he move on? Why was everyone so uptight? It was dreadfully awkward.

"What's going on?" I whispered to Mildred.

"Later," she hissed through gritted teeth.

"OK."

After what seemed like an age, one of the guys rummaged in his pocket and insolently threw a handful of coins across the table toward the taciturn giant, who quickly scooped them from the table and rudely tossed a newspaper back at him. Nobody reached for the paper, yet their disdainful eyes were trained upon it as if it were a rag for scrubbing toilets. I scrutinized each face trying to figure out what seemed to have been lost on me. Only when he had left the building did their countenances relax and the drinking and chatter resumed. Still, no one claimed the newspaper, not even the guy who had paid for it.

Well if no one wants it, I guess I'll take it, I thought as I reached across the table and grabbed it. It was a small newspaper, almost square in shape, about ten pages in length, more like a Sunday newspaper insert than anything. I scanned the title and suddenly all the lights went on, *An Phoblacht* (*The Republic*). The problem was glaringly evident. No one could be seen to support this paper even if they wanted to, neither could one be seen to reject it.

This was the official newspaper of the illegal republican organization, the IRA.

The following morning while using the well-read newspaper to light the fire, I was reminded of last night's bizarre behavior and asked Mildred what all the fuss was about.

"If this goes on week in, week out, why the big production about buying it?" I asked.

"The Gardaí drink in the pubs and are always alert and watching. You wouldn't want to look like you were eager to buy the paper. It's better to withdraw suspicion by behaving like you were forced to purchase it. Everyone up here is guilty until proven innocent, and even then you're still considered tainted," she explained.

Mildred and I spent the weekend discussing our mutual fascination for the north and agreed that living here was like living on a new planet. We were learning the rules as we went along.

Grudgingly, I left Mildred's late on Sunday evening. I was in no hurry home to my lonely life, but as Mother says, "Life is not all fun and games."

It was late in the evening when I left Carndonagh. I chose to go via Derry and the north rather than back through Donegal. Irish roads were laced with potholes, had no lighting or reflective lines, and were a succession of dangerously narrow hairpin bends, while northern roads were pitch-black tarmac with a thick white luminescent stripe down the middle. At night I preferred to join the stripes.

Without a map and driving on pure instinct, I found myself lost in the wilds somewhere between

Derry and Stranorlar. The road was a series of twist and turns with no sign of life anywhere. Anxious to be gone from the eerie emptiness, I increased my speed. On one sharp turn the road ahead was strewn with unraveled sticks of dynamite. I was on top of them in an instant and had no choice but to roll right over them. The reality of what happened hit me like a bolt of lightning.

Oh, my God, I was almost killed! That was dynamite back there!

Panic stricken and with perspiration oozing out my back, my underarms, my forehead, and my palms, I pulled off the road and parked in a gateway. Though desperate for a moment of composure, I knew I had to deny myself the luxury. It would hardly be prudent to be found around the corner a spit away from several rolls of dynamite. A quick pep talk and I was on my way again. All the while my mind was having flashbacks of the maroon candlesticks strewn across the road and the large bundle of them taped together by the ditch. Who was it set for? Was a patrol due soon? Was it a trap for an individual or the army? My mind buzzed, recalling the endless lectures about not rolling over anything on the road in the north: a wire, a paper bag, a rope, a water hose, an empty Chinese carton—nothing was safe. All items were suspect. Then I burst into nervous laughter while contemplating what my friends would think if I told them I had driven right over unexploded dynamite! I should have collected a few for proof.

Having found the main road, I sped toward the border. Thankfully the border guys just waved me on. I couldn't wait to tell Mildred about my latest escapade.

I'll have to return to Carndonagh soon! I mused to myself.

ENTERING FREE DEERY

The North of Ireland was a very volatile place in the mid 1980s. Mildred and I were enthralled by the constant action and read everything we could in an effort to understand our new environment. We also took every opportunity to explore the most notorious places.

Derry is a city with a rich ancient past and a tumultuous recent history. It is also renowned for its religious divide, where neighborhoods are separated into Catholic and Protestant. Even the city's name changes depending upon religious affiliation! Protestants call it Londonderry, while Catholics simply call it Derry. Londonderry presumes ignorance; English or Protestant, while identifying the city as Derry, assumes Republican, Catholic, or both, and possibly a terrorist, but at the very least a rabble-rouser.

Mildred and I were particularly interested in the infamous Catholic communities of the Bogside and

Creggan. Nightly news indicated continuous contentious actions in both estates. The Bogside, a sprawling Catholic tenement just outside the city walls, is renowned for many historical events, including the Battle of the Bogside and Bloody Sunday, and for its numerous murals and graffiti, the most famous being the freestanding gable announcing the entrance to the Bogside. This brilliant white gable wall announces in bold black capital letters: "You are now entering Free Derry." Other painted gables throughout the Bogside are stunningly skillful, yet poignantly provocative. Tourists continue to admire and photograph this artwork. The Creggan, similarly, is a sprawling housing estate situated upon a hill on the outskirts of Derry, constructed with the expressed purpose of housing Catholic working class. These communities were broadcasted globally as unrelenting hotbeds of rebellious activity. We simply had to experience them firsthand.

On the morning of our departure, Mildred pronounced quite emphatically, "I'll only go if we take your car."

"Great," I said. "You just don't want yours hijacked."

"Exactly," she agreed shamelessly.

Cars were regularly hijacked and used as car bombs or burning blockades on city streets. My Southern registered car was particularly at risk. I really wanted to visit Derry and was willing to take a chance with my jalopy. We hit the road. The lads at the border waved us on, no stopping, no interrogation, no document verification, not a bother at all, just a wave of the hand signaling, "Off you go ladies."

The frequency of burnings and bombings endured by Derry over the years deemed it a miracle this Irish city still boasted its original walls. Ghost lots, crumbling burnt out ruins, and barbed-wire fencing decorated the city center, while housing estates littered the perimeter. At night, businesses sealed up tight, drawing silver metal shutters across their shop fronts, adding a sterile, military aspect to the city center. I found safe public parking mid-city on the raised foundation of a bombed out building transformed into a state-of-the art parking lot. My car was perfectly safe until 6 p.m., closing time.

We trudged up a steep hill toward the city gates, which led directly to the Bogside. Our first sighting was the famous white gable announcing that we were now entering Free Derry. A heavily armed convoy sat nervously on the edge, surveying the neighborhood but not daring to enter. Conscious of military eyes, we walked around the gable afraid to take any pictures or draw too much attention to ourselves. If the military mistook our cameras for guns, we could be shot on the spot. We had heard propaganda of youths yielding paintbrushes encountering this fate. With a reflexive eye on the military, we cautiously edged deeper into the Bogside and began walking between the houses admiring the gable graffiti. Being teachers we marveled at the artistic abilities of these unknown artists, but again were too intimidated by the military scrutiny, and the suspicious locals, to capture them in photograph.

"I'm wild thirsty," complained Mildred as we passed the Bogside Bar. "I'd love a drink."

"Fine, but couldn't you wait until we get back to the city? These locals are often very wary of newcomers. They might be hostile to us invading their space."

"Oh, for goodness sake!"

She pulled open the door and boldly strutted inside. Like a suck calf I followed closely behind and slunk into a corner seat hoping to blend in with the woodwork. We were the only women in the place. Mildred marched straight to the bar and ordered. Fortunately, the men were so rapt in their dart competition that we were completely off their radar. The palpable physical energy, passion, language use, power, and personalities of those men were spectacularly vibrant and quite intimidating. Though frightened, I was also impressed. Thankfully Mildred satiated her thirst rather quickly and we were out of there.

Having walked about twenty minutes back toward the city, I realized I had left my coat in the bar. Furiously angry at my own stupidity, I marched back to the bar, stomped inside, and went directly to my seat hoping to retrieve the missing coat. Of course it wasn't there. All eyes were on me as the barman came out from behind the bar flaying my coat high above his head. He did a slow motion hip walk toward me. Every one clapped and jeered. He grabbed me by the shoulders and spun me around till my back was facing him. Then he dressed me into my coat, spun me back around facing him and buttoned me up to the last buttonhole, patted me on the head, and said, "There you are now, lassie."

The whole bar applauded, whistled, and cheered. It was a forceful yet friendly crowd. Bowing low to the ground, I thanked the barman, then bid the crowd good day.

At six o'clock I moved my car from the city parking lot to a parking spot outside a pub directly opposite the Bogside. For supper we savored tea and cakes at Austin's, the oldest department store in Derry, famous for high-end shopping and cream-filled pastries.

"Let's meet some natives," suggested Mildred as we sauntered back toward the car.

"What have you in mind?"

"We could hit the pubs."

"How will we know where to go? What if we end up in a loyalist bar or worse?"

"You're parked right outside a pub practically in the Bogside. It's a safe bet. We can start there."

"OK."

The barman grinned from ear to ear when I ordered, and he immediately asked, "What part of the South are yous from?"

"Cork and Tipperary," I replied

Of course he had cousins and friends in each place. We chit-chatted for a while as he poured our drinks. Then he asked, "Do you have a car with you?"

"Yes."

"Is it a Southern reg?'

"Of course. Why?"

"Where did you park it?"

"Right outside the door," I replied.

"Hmmm," he hummed, shaking his head. "Not the best idea."

"Why not?"

"There's been riots all week, and with that Southern registration it will be stolen and used as a road block."

"No one would take my car!" I exclaimed. "It's a banger."

"Them's the best kind for setting on fire," he scoffed.

"What am I to do?"

"Pull it around back. Jack here will open the gate," he offered.

I drove the car around the back, and Jack, the other barman, opened the gate signaling me inside. My car was the safest car in all Derry that night. Mildred smiled smugly at me, and I knew what she was thinking.

"That's why I didn't bring my car!"

We were immediately joined at the bar by two elderly men in their mid-thirties. They began telling us all about the troubles. Being startled by our absolute ignorance, they felt it their duty to teach us the history of Derry City. They recounted stories of Bloody Sunday, where thirteen were gunned down in a civil rights march. That was in 1972, only about ten years ago. They warned us to leave Derry early or our car would be in danger. There had been riots all week, and tonight would be no exception.

"God, I'd love to see a riot," Mildred said.

I agreed.

"We'll take you," the guys offered.

"Time to move away, Mildred, or we will be paying them for the tour and not in cash," I whispered in Irish.

We excused ourselves from our educators and cozied into an alcove where we began discussing the day's events.

It was not long before two dapper, handsome, well-dressed young men begged leave to join us. One, Con, was tall and blond and reminded me of a younger version of Robert Redford. The other young man, Jerry, was short and dark like Al Pacino. These lads were closer to our age than the two at the bar and far more attractive. We accepted their offer without hesitation. Our suitors enthusiastically began educating two naive, pretty girls from the South, and we were the perfect audience rapt in absolute fascination, stroking their eager egos. Upon closing the four of us left for the Embassy Disco, but were refused entry because the doors closed at 11 p.m. sharp. Priests acted as bouncers, and they were quite rigid about the rules. There was no sweet-talking them into letting us in. We tried New York, New York, instead. That was a blast, and we danced till closing time with plans to attend a party afterward.

Full of energy we scampered down the street right into a mêlée of RUC vans maneuvering into position all over The Strand Road. Entries and exits were barricaded in anticipation of another riot. A crowd assembled outside the Embassy Disco Hall.

"Looks like another riot tonight," Jerry commented nonchalantly.

"Aye," replied Con.

"There's going to be a riot," Mildred exclaimed excitedly. "I'd love to see a riot. Can we stay?"

"We'll have to move out of harm's way," Jerry cautioned as he gently ushered us down the street toward the police barricade.

"We're safer behind these guys if there's a riot," he explained.

"Do you really think there'll be a riot, seriously?" I asked.

"Well, there's been rioting every weekend now for a month. Looks like they're going at it again tonight."

"Wow, a riot! This is so exciting," we eejits proclaimed almost in unison. The lads pulled us behind the police barricade.

"Sure, we can hardly see a thing from here," I complained.

"If that crowd flares up, you'll be glad you're at this end. They have no ammunition, but these guys do. This is the end you want to be standing at if it all goes wrong," Jerry warned.

The crowds spilled out of bars, dance halls, picture shows, and discos. Rambunctiously they raced toward a long line that had gathered at the end of the street opposite the police and us. The mob swelled and grew over the next thirty minutes. Soon it was the width of the street and about ten people deep. The human wave growled and pulsed, but failed to advance.

"What's the matter?" Mildred asked. "Why aren't they attacking?"

"They're waiting for a signal or for someone to throw the first stone or petrol bomb. Then they'll roar into action."

We watched as the crowd jeered and taunted, swelled and swayed, but it never burst forth into a riot. Little by little the edges frayed, leaving isolated clusters scattered up and down The Strand. We were utterly disappointed. Our consolation price was a fascinating view of the riot police disassembling their gear.

"What was that all about? Not a single shot fired!" Mildred complained.

"Maybe they're getting fed up of the weekly riots," Con explained.

"That's just our luck! What about next weekend?"

"Aye, if you want to," Con agreed.

"Same time, same place?" Jerry piped in.

"We'll be there," I promised.

"In your car!" Mildred added.

Gabrielle Ní Mheachair

SAOIRSE GO LUATH

A week later we went back to the pub. The barman let me park in my usual spot. The Derry boys eagerly awaited our arrival. Jerry and Con were extremely proud of their city and its heritage. They boasted that Derry was the best-dressed city in Ireland and its women the prettiest.

"Remember Dana of the Eurovision Song Contest?" they reminded.

They went on to list famous Derry models of whom we hadn't an iota, but we played along to appease our generous chaperones.

After closing time we hiked up a hill from which one could see the whole city spread out like a colorful psychedelic carpet glowing in the ink-black night. Using the lighted city as a backdrop, they recounted a lively, personal interpretation of Derry's history. Pointing to the empty stand where a statue of Lord Walker stood before the IRA blew him up.

"Walker, they said, sold the keys of Derry to the Catholics for a bap [a drink]," Jerry proclaimed.

We strode along the path where, "the Protestants walked as they threw pennies to the Bogside Catholics." They called our attention to the main army barracks, the police station, bombed-out buildings, streets, estates, and pubs—distinguishing between which to avoid and which to frequent. We visited the city's largest police station on one side of the river. It was like a decorated Christmas tree, only instead of tinsel it was draped in barbed wire. The doors and windows were shuttered. Foot patrols paced up and down the street outside, while soldiers peered through narrow slits at the top of tall turrets scrutinizing the surrounding county. Mildred grew up on a farm in Cork, and not a Garda for miles. I grew up surrounded by hundreds of them, all innocent young lads, more like Boy Scouts than policemen. The Derry military was fascinating, fine uniformed bodies weighed down by an array of guns, obscure equipment, and bulletproof jackets, more like human turtles concealing their true selves inside a shell of armor. Though their drills captivated us, the bored boys pulled away, routing us back to The Strand to check out the riot situation. Vicious disappointment ensued. Last week's performance was repeated almost exactly. Neither a stone nor a gum spit was cast in the direction of the police. Again, riots all week, but when we showed up, nothing.

"Maybe you guys should live here full-time; then we'd have peace," Con joked.

"Yea," begged Jerry, who obviously liked Mildred. "You could move in with me!"

We snickered. Jerry was obviously too young for her. But it was flattering nonetheless.

"Now what?" Mildred asked.

"No riot, no action. It's late. I want tea and cake."

I had a habit of inviting myself back to people's houses for tea and cake. Then I raided the place "bishop style."

"We can't go to my house," Jerry blurted out nervously.

"Why not?"

"The mother!"

"Ah, will she still be up?"

"Something like that!"

Con immediately proffered, "I'll take you to my house."

I'd swear he took us all over the city so we could never remember how to find his place again. We walked for miles uphill, miles downhill, through a million different housing estates before finally coming to a nondescript council house where he announced, "This is it!"

The living room floor was lined with sleeping bags. Children ranging from ages eight to sixteen raised their heads, took one look at us, and went right back to sleep. No introductions.

"Slumber party?" Mildred asked.

"Sort of," Con responded.

There's no way that range of ages are having an overnight party, I mused, but kept my mouth shut. I wanted the tea and chocolate biscuits he had promised.

Con ushered us into the kitchen, where we plonked our toiled, weary bodies on kitchen chairs. Jerry plugged the kettle in while Con rummaged in the cupboard, producing a brand-new sealed tin of biscuits. I snatched it right out of his hands, tore off the tape, and sat down as happy as a first communicant with a purse full of money. I began stuffing my face with all the chocolate ones and failed to notice Con leaving the room. Cumbersomely he shuffled back into the kitchen carting an armload of wooden objects. Item-by-item he unloaded his burden, placing each piece reverently on the table before us. There was an assortment of inlays made from blond wood, possibly oak; trays, plaques, and statuettes all representing the republican themes of incarceration, struggle, independence, and freedom. Mildred and I were gob smacked at such magnificent craftsmanship! And justifiably so. These were sacred objects. There was no touching allowed, admire from a distance only! I wanted the inlay harp so badly I would have stolen it given half the chance. It was the most beautiful piece of woodwork I had ever seen. Each corner had a single, spiky barb inlayed with a darker wood. When I looked at it, I felt, pain. A stringed harp, our national emblem, adorned the center. No sweet music emanated from its barbed-wire strings, just the mournful cry of a tear-stained youth imprisoned behind them, "Saoirse go Luath!" ("Freedom soon!" or, "Soon we will be free!") was inlayed underneath.

"Did you make these?" I asked Con, hoping to beg one from him if he had.

"Nope," he replied curtly.

"Well who did?"

"My father."

"Wow! He's mighty talented."

I noticed Jerry get shifty on his feet, and figured something was amiss.

"Does he sell them?"

"Nope. He can't."

"Why not? I'd buy one. I love the inlay of the harp in different-colored woods. It's fab!"

"Well, they're not for sale."

"I'd be happy to pay for the harp."

"They're not mine to sell."

"Ask you dad to make one for me."

"Can't do that either."

Con glanced at Jerry as if asking for permission, then enormously embarrassed he pronounced, "Look, he's in jail, OK?"

Silence ensued as we tried to get our brain around this statement. I never knew anyone who went to jail in modern times. In the olden times my ancestors went to jail for rebelling against the Brits, or land agitation, but that sort of stuff was something you boasted about. It was a badge of honor. The North of Ireland was different. Though the same sentiments were at play, the same rules didn't apply. One of us asked why he was in jail, but I don't remember which one.

"He's a nationalist."

"Well, we kind of guessed that from the woodwork," I responded.

"Sorry about your father. Will he get out soon?" Mildred asked kindly.

"He's in for life, but they're appealing," Con replied pathetically.

"What did he do?"

"Nothing. He's innocent."

"Well what is he in for then?"

He claimed his father was one of the 1994 Birmingham Six.

"He went to prison nine years ago with all his teeth, sound in body and mind, but now he is blind in one eye and has a set of false teeth. He's a Special Security "A" prisoner and therefore, denied any privileges. He spends his time creating these wonderful works of art."

Having heard his story, the harp plaque took on a whole new meaning. Con's eyes held the sadness of the inlayed, imprisoned weeping child. His house was Ireland: five fatherless girls; a lonely mother, almost widowed; and Con, a lonely son playing the role of a brother and father! I begged to purchase the piece, but there was no way Con was parting with it. It became very awkward in the kitchen after that. Thankfully, Mildred loudly checked the time and decided we needed to get going. The lads agreed to walk us back to the bar. We took a much shorter route this time. On our way back Con informed us that times were really bad right now, because the republican prisoners were protesting for political status in the prison where his father was, a rooftop or blanket protest or something like that. He insinuated that his father would suffer consequences for these actions. We didn't want to display our total lack of compassion by asking him to explain. Sure enough his story was confirmed with news reports on British and Irish television. The prison revolt was called a blanket protest. We returned the following weekend hoping to hook up with our Derry boys, but they weren't at the pub. We asked the barman about them. He hadn't seen them all week. We decided to drive to Con's house and track them down. Clever Mildred remembered the landmarks they had pointed out on our way back from his house. We rang the doorbell a dozen times, but no one answered. We walked all the way around the perimeter, peering through the ground-floor windows. The entire house had been cleaned out. There wasn't a stick of furniture left in the place.

Later it was reported his whole family had been ghosted, or secretly whipped away in the dead of night, for fear of military repercussions due to his father's alleged political inclinations. We never heard from or of him again. Many times over the years we wondered about his family and his father.

As a result of our meeting with Con and Jerry, our Derry gentlemen, Mildred and I greatly sympathized with the victims of the troubles.

Note: *The Birmingham Six appealed their sentence. In 1991 their convictions were quashed. It was agreed that the police did indeed fabricate and suppress evidence at the first (1975) trial. It was also found that confessions were forced under duress and torture. The Birmingham Six were released on March 14, 1991, after sixteen and a half years behind bars.*

Gabrielle Ní Mheachair

THE REAL THING

Having failed to find a riot in Derry, the next best thing was to attend an IRA funeral, which were often broadcast on the news. We fantasized about standing in the crowd, watching men wearing black balaclavas fire volleys over the casket while the army stood by helpless, hemmed out by the tightly crammed crowd. Oh, the very idea was exhilarating! Mildred found the perfect opportunity in the latest copy of *An Phoblacht.* It seems providence was listening to our foolish plans. A contentious controversy exploded globally, questioning Britain's shoot-to-kill policy in Northern Ireland. Did it, or did it not, exist? No one knew for sure, but both sides had definite opinions. The event that triggered this debate was the shooting of a motorcyclist on his way into Altnagelvin Hospital in Derry City.

A young man sped along the winding driveway of Altnagelvin Hospital on his flashy motor cycle, blissfully ignorant of the fact the military were concealed on the grounds armed and trigger ready. As soon as he whizzed within range of their hidden positions, they opened fire. He lost control of the bike and fell off. His contorted, blood-spattered body lay sprawled on the driveway riddled with bullet holes. The military claimed they had been given a tip that the victim was on a Republican mission to "take care" of a hospital patient. Hence, they got ready to "take care" of their business, responding with the "shoot-to-kill" policy that didn't exist. It was also claimed that having searched the dead body, the victim was found to be carrying a gun. Republicans claimed that no such orders were given and the motor cyclist was simply visiting a relative in hospital, where he was cold-bloodily gunned down in broad daylight. Mildred was on the phone, excitedly announcing that she had found our event. The funeral of the Altnagelvin victim was scheduled for the coming weekend. We would be among the mourners. This promised to be the most notorious funeral of the year.

Derry was mobbed, and Mildred became impatient because we lost a lot of time finding a safe parking spot. It was looking like we would be late for the funeral.

"Just park it anywhere. It'll be fine."

"It's my car, and I need to be sure it is safe. Next time bring your car," I snapped.

Following local directions, we made our way into the Creggan, a sprawling, hilltop, Catholic housing estate outside the city walls. Grid rows of identical houses stretched before us for what seemed like miles. We entered this concrete geometric maze using the church spire as our compass and ultimate destination.

"Looks like we missed a good fight too," Mildred complained.

The curbs were littered with glass shards and flaming broken bottles.

"Petrol bombs," she added authoratively. "Probably still burning on the sugar."

"Sugar?"

"Yep, someone told me they put sugar in the petrol bombs so they stick to their target. It's clever isn't it?"

Clever, yes, thought I, as my nerves began to tingle. *Bombs, sugar, fire, flames! This was the real thing and we were walking straight into the middle of it.*

Our lively progress toward the spire was suddenly blocked by a roughly constructed barricade of toppled electric and telephone poles, mounds of wooden crates, pallets, and other waste timbers.

"Looks like the road ahead is blocked. We'll have to go back," I said, being a coward.

Mildred ignored my suggestion and gestured to a side street.

"That looks too unsteady for us to climb over it. Let's just cut down that street?"

We backtracked and hooked up with a parallel street, only to find it too was blocked. This time a hijacked vehicle formed the centerpiece of the blockade and the side spans were loaded with trash, tires, and shards of timber. A large crowd milled to and fro as they continued construction. Avoiding an encounter with the busy crowd, we backtracked again and tried another parallel to find that it too was blocked. This time a mini-bus formed the centerpiece. A few wooden boards and tangled debris had been built on either side. Clearly, the builders had left in a hurry, their task unfinished. We successfully clambered over the lowest side, surveyed the horizon for our compass, and persisted toward the spire of Saint Mary's Church.

Suddenly there appeared before us, as if dropped from the sky, a huge bear of a man wearing a black balaclava and military fatigues. He stopped for but a second, looked straight through us like a clear glass window, searched left, then right, got his bearings, and darted across the street. Skillfully as an Olympic athlete, he swung himself over a small garden gate, rushed toward the hall door, pushed himself inside, and was gone behind a swiftly slammed door. It all happened so quickly we were rooted to the sidewalk with shock. Almost instantaneously a charge of gun-toting military pounded toward us like stampeding antelope. They came from both ends of the street, surrounding us on all sides. They too jumped the low estate wall, but rushed around the house toward the backyard. I wet myself.

Having had the wits and piss scared out of me, I wanted to give up, retreat, and go home. I had undeniably and unabashedly lost my nerve.

"Mildred, I want to go home," I almost cried. "I don't think I have the stomach for this."

"We've come this far. We're not going back now. Anyway we're almost there," she ordered.

Mildred was right. The church was in plain view, a few more yards and we would crest the top of the hill. Reluctantly I pressed on only to find the largest, most tightly packed crowd I had ever seen pushing and shoving toward the church door anxious to be part of this moment in history. Petite Mildred thrust her way through the multitude, with me trailing behind attached to the hem of her sweater. At the main chapel doors the crowd was so firmly packed it was impossible to move let alone get inside.

"Let's just move to the edge of the crowd," I begged fearful my claustrophobic tendencies would kick in. With immense difficulty and many a raging stare, we managed to extricate ourselves from the throng of bystanders and huddle on the edge. Thankful for fresh air and physical freedom, I breathed a sigh of relief and sat on a low brick wall behind me. Mildred joined me. From our vantage point at the top of the hill we scanned the housing estate sprawled below us. Imagine our alarm when we spotted a gang of balaclava-clad men fleeing through the mazed housing estate pursued by a detachment of soldiers. They dashed across streets, into houses, out into backyards, over fences, and across streets, on and on through the next house, and the next house, until they had made their way safely through the estate avoiding capture. The military couldn't enter the houses without a search warrant. They had to go the long way around each house and call for reinforcements. It wasn't long before we also noticed the growing police presence furtively tightening its circle around the crowd. And we were on the wrong side of that circle. Armored cars and tank-like vehicles with revolving turrets were settling into place at the base of the hill.

"Mildred, do you see what I see? It's going to get pretty tense here when the coffin comes out. I don't like the feel of this place, and we're right in the middle of it. We're surrounded. What if the shoot-to-kill policy is for real?"

Fortunately, our predicament was not lost on her. Thank God she valued her life more than her sport and agreed to retreat. Content to admit I was a full-fledged coward, I didn't need an excuse to withdraw. We plotted our departure, picking the most direct route from the hilltop, which meant scrambling over several barricades as we briskly strode down the hill toward my car in silence.

That night we sat among friends watching the news. The funeral went off without incident. Scenes from the event flashed across the screen. Barricades we had scaled were now engulfed in flames, keeping the police at bay so the people could mourn their loss in peace.

"We were there!" we exclaimed with pride.

UNWELCOME HOUSEGUESTS

One would think we Southern girls would have learned that nothing good comes from our rash behavior. Ach no! Our appetite for trouble grew. We decided to take on Belfast. Belfast was the epicenter of the Northern universe. Moira, a dear friend and college student at Queens, was our contact there. Despite her efforts to dissuade us, we invited ourselves to her place for the next long weekend. Mildred and I were coming, whether she wanted us or not. As usual, my car was conscripted for the trip.

We arrived in Belfast at the front door of a typical estate house, with two rooms and a kitchen downstairs and three bedrooms upstairs. Moira made it quite clear that it was a Protestant estate and we were to keep our Catholic ways in check. Mildred and I couldn't give a hoot about such things; we were busy preening ourselves for the pub and disco.

"There are no discos on a Friday night. Friday night is picture night," Moira announced.

"Sure that's grand," we agreed. "Pub then pictures!"

"No, its pictures then pub."

Neither of us cared what we did as long as we got to see what Belfast had to offer, day or night.

We dolled ourselves up in our finest regalia.

"Right, where's the nearest bus stop? What number do we get? How much will it be?"

It was a bit of a shock to us when the girls announced we weren't taking the bus. They didn't like taking busses.

"What about black taxis?"

They shunned black taxis. There were no trains or subways, so it was shanks mare or my car.

"I'm not taking my car into the heart of Belfast at night. And if ye refuse to take a taxi or bus, I don't want to hear a word about sore feet later on," I said, more concerned for myself than anyone else. Fortunately the picture hall wasn't far down the road, and we stopped at a local pub on the way home for a wee rest. Mildred and I were seriously disappointed at how dull Moira and her friends were. There was no action anywhere. Everything they did was calculated, safe, and boring. We were even home before midnight!

"Well at least we can tour the city tomorrow. We'll do it ourselves," Mildred suggested.

"Absolutely!" I agreed.

We needn't have worried; no one wanted to come with us anyway. It was obvious we were unwelcome houseguests.

The following morning, I was awakened from a deep sleep by loud banging on my bedroom door and hysterical females downstairs ranting and raving about police out front.

"There's police all over the place," someone panicked.

Police? I thought and jumped out of bed all excited at the thought of seeing some action, or at the very least some fine bodies! I rushed over to the window and tore open the curtains. Sure enough, there they were, down on the street below my window, a mêlée of policemen and a fleet of armored cars blocking the road. Gun-toting soldiers in an array of beret colors were staring directly at the house. It was exhilarating. I scampered downstairs to find the Northern girls lined up along the narrow hallway ranting and raving about the police on their very own door step.

"It's your car," Stacy pointed at me accusingly. "You and your Southern registration! Someone must have called it in."

"Sure, what of it?" I said, turning on my heels as I headed for the door.

"You're not going out looking like that?" she warned.

I opened the door and walked straight outside, tired eyed, tousled haired, bare footed, sporting flannel pajamas, and braless. I could hear the girls behind me scurry to the sitting-room window for a better look.

"What's up?" I asked the policeman nearest me. All the while I was spotting the lineup for the cutest ones.

"Is this your car?"

"'Tis."

"Do you mind if we ask you a few questions?"

"Fire away," I said, "but can we do it in the police car. I'm frozen solid."

I was escorted to the police car parked directly behind mine. A cutie opened the door and politely ushered me into the backseat. Two hunks sat in the front. I giggled at the thought of the girls peering out the window and going berserk thinking I was being arrested. The officers and I had a great chat. I told them who we were, Mildred and I. How this was our first time in Belfast. They gave me pointers about the safest parking spots, must-see places, and places to avoid. They were so nice! We even made a date to meet at the disco that night. After what must have seemed like an age to the onlookers, I stepped out of the police car and strolled back inside. The patrol left as noisily as they had entered, and peace was once again restored to the sleepy Saturday morning housing estate.

"What was all that about?" the girls asked as they crammed in the hallway to greet my return.

"My car! You were right. That Southern registration gets their attention every time."

"Well, we're not going into the city with you today," Moira announced bluntly.

"That's fine, because we're going up the Falls for some photos."

The Falls Road is the most famous Republican and Catholic neighborhood in Belfast. Stories of the Falls made the nightly news. A trip to Belfast without a stroll down the Falls Road would be like a going to Rome and not visiting the Vatican. Besides, we needed bragging points.

"You could get shot taking pictures up there," she warned, "You better be careful."

"We will."

Mildred was grinning from ear to ear enjoying the girls' reaction. We were turning their world upside down. We thought we were the clever ones, but they knew we were stupid idiots messing where we had no idea at all.

The suspicious eyes of the Falls Road residents were more threatening than any other place we had dared to go. Women stood in open doorways scanning pedestrians as they sauntered up and down the street. Gangs of sullen youths lolled on windowsills outside local pubs, leering at us as we passed by. Men rushed past us on busy errands, but always made a point to take a second look. Struggling with apprehension I managed to get a few gable photos. The glaring intimidation halted our progress, and we decided to check out Sandy Road in East Belfast, the Protestant equivalent of the Falls. In direct contrast to the Falls, this estate was as vacant as a graveyard on a cold winter's day, abandoned without a soul in sight. All doors were shut tight. No children played on the roads. No youths lolled on windowsills. Even the military were absent. And to top it off, the gable graffiti was sparse and lackluster. Disenchanted, we returned to the city.

"Where do you think everyone was?" I wondered aloud.

"Maybe all at work?" Mildred suggested.

"But the Falls was full of people!"

"Maybe they're all unemployed. Isn't that one of their complaints, equal employment opportunities?"

"I s'pose, but it was still kind of weird how opposite both roads were."

Our trip around Belfast was without incident. All in all Belfast was just like Derry, a broken-down city with a huge military presence, control zones, roadblocks, army checkpoints, body frisks, handbag checks, and constant security. Disappointed, we returned to the girls that evening. They were not interested in our observations and fielded all questions. However, they were excited about the disco. That promised better relations and results.

ABDUCTION

Note: *Ulster Military Force, UMF, is used instead of the real military name to protect identities. To my knowledge there is no such military group as the UMF.*

We girls spruced up for the disco with flashy makeup, high heels, shimmery dresses, and not an ounce of sense among us. Mildred and I insisted on a black taxi. We had walked enough for one day. Reluctantly the girls conceded and agreed to take advantage of the free ride. I guess they realized, as Mother used to say, "There's strength in numbers." The taxi deposited us at the pub. Tensions between us relaxed as we sat around the table drinking sodas and exchanging stories. By now Mildred and I knew Northern topics were off-limits; instead we complained about our jobs, reminisced about the good old days, and chit-chatted about life in general. When the pub closed, we were laughing happily like lifelong friends, linking arms four abreast across the street and giggling all the way to the disco.

Even today I fail to understand the attraction of the dance hall. Loud music. Flashing lights. Frantic passions. Men and women pushing and shoving like cattle packed into a yard. Spilled drinks. Stale perfume. Cigarette smoke and sweat all swirling about, fusing to nose hairs and clothes. Boorish men trying their luck at the prettiest girls, then dropping their standards lower and lower as the night wears on. The humiliation of girls standing in neat rows like glass, candy jars on a shelf, hoping to be selected for the taste test, with the last lady standing in absolute degradation and ultimate humiliation. Why we subject ourselves to this mortification, night after night, year after year, is beyond me. More incredible is that we spent large sums of hard-earned money to undergo this demeaning experience. Are we that desperate for men? I stood on that candy shelf all night long, enduring gawking men parading by and shaking their heads in an effort to dismiss my image from their minds before they moved on to the next girl in line. There was comfort in knowing that Moira, Stacy, and Mildred all suffered similar fates. Tonight's disco was a massive waste of energy, effort, time, and money. And much to my utter disappointment, the RUC guys who had promised to meet us never showed up.

Walking across the parking lot toward the taxi line we ran into a bunch of guys who said they were going to a party. Boldly we asked if we could join them. They seemed excited at the prospect of our company and offered to take us with them. We piled into their economy-size car and sat on each other's lap. They gave us the night tour of Belfast. None of us has any idea where we were, and no one seemed to be paying attention. After what seemed like an age of giddy, giggling, laughing, and verbal bantering, the car stopped and we found ourselves parked outside a newly constructed prefabricated building similar to a military billet. For the longest time no one made any attempt to leave the car. Mildred noticed the absence of other cars, commotion, or music. Either we were early or there was no party.

"So where's this party?" she piped up.

"We're waiting for the guys in the other car to show up."

"I need to go to the little girl's room," Stacy announced.

"I'll go with you," I suggested. "Where is it?"

"In that building right there. You can't miss it."

"I'm cramped and sore," Mildred complained. "I need to get out of this car and stretch my legs."

"We have a great obstacle course here," one of the guys suggested, "Want to do it?"

Mildred, Miss Athlete, couldn't pass up an opportunity to prove her prowess. Moira and two of the guys joined her, while Stacy and I went to the bathroom. The other two sat in the car.

One step inside the building Stacy stopped dead in her tracks and announced, "This is a military barracks."

"So?"

"Look at the bulletin boards all the way down the hallway."

I began reading the bulletin boards and discovered that we were in a UMF barracks.

"It's a UMF training camp, the Ulster Military Force," Stacy shrieked in panic.

"What's wrong with the UMF?" I asked innocently.

"Oh, my God! We're dead! We're dead!" she wailed. Then she began to flail her arms in panic. Finally, she gripped her head like it was about to explode and she needed to hold it tight so the pieces would be contained.

"What are we going to do?" she begged. "We're dead, we're dead, we're dead," she said over and over again.

"Calm down, will you? We're fine. Shhh! Someone will hear you."

"You've no idea, do you? God, you guys are so stupid. Do you know that?" she went on.

I looked at her blankly. My mind suggested she was overreacting again. She obviously had issues with uniforms. This morning it was the police, and now it was the UMF. I watched as Stacy crumbled into a heap on the floor. She covered her face in her hands and began to sob.

Woah! I thought, *This must be bad.*

"Stacy, calm down. Talk to me. Come on. Get up. Let's go to the bathroom. I'm bursting to pee. Come on," I coaxed.

I pulled her to her feet, and we made it to the bathroom in silence. We tinkled, washed our hands, and set about leaving. Before we got to the door, though, she stopped, stood up straight, and glared at me with panic in her bright-blue eyes.

"We've got to get out of here! Our honor and our lives are in danger. These are bad guys."

"OK, I get it. But calm down. Now tell me exactly who are the UMF?"

"They're murderers and rapists, and they hate Catholics," she spat.

There was silence between us for a second.

"I hardly think they're going to murder all four of us," I replied trying to calm her, but my own anxiety was building.

"Haven't you heard the stories of what they do for fun? Och! How could you? You grew up in the South. You know nothing of life up here. We're in real danger. Those UMFs are out there just waiting for their friends to get back, and we are their party!"

Stacy began pacing the hallway then snapped, "Don't you get it? We can't get out. We're in here illegally. No one knows where we are. And no one will ever believe us. We're trapped."

All the lights in my head went on; the alarm bells joined them. I realized what Stacy was saying made sense. Regardless of who these guys were, we were their party. We needed to escape.

"We have to find the others and tell them what's going on!" I said.

"How can we do that? They'll hear us." Stacy replied.

"Let's go back to the car and pretend to nothing. I'll tell Mildred what's up, and we'll work from there."

"OK, but we have to get out of here. Now!"

We sauntered back to the car as casually as we could. The two guys sat chatting in the front. Shrieks and laughter told us the girls were still out there with the other lads doing the assault course. We chit-chatted with the guys for a while, and then I brazenly asked the driver for his ID. Reluctantly he showed me his card, keeping his thumb firmly on the middle where UMF was embossed in bold letters. I snatched it out of his hand and took a good look. Sure enough, he was UMF. Stacy was right. We were in trouble.

"I'm hungry. Let's get the girls and go to the chippers," I suggested.

"I'm starving too. I'd kill for a burger and chips right now," Stacy proclaimed as she jumped out of the car to go find the girls. I followed her, and the guys followed me. Stacy began yelling Moira's name, and soon the girls were at our side. I hooked Mildred's arm, and pulling her forward alongside me, slowly led the pack back toward the car.

"We're for the chippers and then back for the party," I announced loudly for the benefit of all. Then I whispered to Mildred, in Irish, that we were in a bit of a predicament. Once she understood the plan, she donned her fighting mode and almost dragged me to the car.

Much to our relief the guys thought the chippers was a good idea. Soon we found ourselves outside the compound and on our way back to Belfast. Moira was still in the dark with no clue as to the danger we were in, and there was no way to communicate our distress to her. She spoke no Irish and no French. We would have to team up, Mildred and Stacy, Moira and me.

"I want to go to the Roma chippers on Main Street," Stacy pouted. "They have the best chips in town."

"I hope they're made from real spuds and not those fake, frozen, fast-food ones," I said.

"The Roma buys from local farmers. They wash, peel, and chop the potatoes by hand. They're guaranteed to be big, fat, salty spuds with lashings of vinegar," Stacy confirmed.

I was salivating at the thought of such delicious potatoes and began placing mental orders: fish and chips, sausage and chips, burger and chips, curry chips, chicken and chips, and so on. The guys parked on the street right outside the Roma.

"You girls stay in the car, and we'll get your orders," one guy suggested.

"I'm coming inside. I want to see what they have," Mildred announced boldly as she made for the door. Taking her lead I shoved the other girls out behind her. While we stood on the street straightening our dresses, I pulled Moira toward me and whispered, "We have a problem, these guys are UMF."

Moira turned pale and seemed to stumble in her high heels. I didn't need to utter another word. It was obvious that name sent shivers down her spine too.

"What are we going to do?" she almost screeched.

"Follow our lead. We have a plan. Just try to act normal."

The lads lined up along the counter and read the bulletin board menu from there. We girls hung back by the shop window, pretending to be taking our time deciding what we wanted.

"The minute they go to place their order we'll make a run for it. I have a friend who lives near here," Stacy whispered through gritted teeth.

All four of us took one look at the guys, then at the door, and almost immediately we were out of there running down the street as fast as we could in tight shirts and high heels. Stacy ran ahead, leading the way.

"God, I hope she knows where she is going," Mildred said as we galloped through the streets of Belfast in the wee hours of the morning.

"The guys! They're behind us in the car," Moira wailed.

Stacy cut down a side street, and we stumbled along behind her as fast as we could. My heart beat loudly in my chest. I looked around and saw their car turn into the street behind us. *They really do mean business*, I thought. I was truly frightened now.

They were gaining on us. Stacy, still running, reached down and pulled of her shoes; we followed suit. At this point we didn't care about torn hose, or sore feet. We had to out run that car. Up and down streets, one ways and two ways, we raced, the car in hot pursuit.

"Stacy, do you have any idea where you are?" Moira snapped.

"It's here somewhere. We're in the right area of town. I'm sure of it."

We found ourselves in a Georgian neighborhood. All the houses looked the same, red-black walls in the dark of night, creepy steep stairs to blood-red Georgian doors, basement windows that winked behind prisonlike rails. Stacy charged up the steps of one of them and pounded violently on the door, all the while yelling, "Liz, Liz, Liz, it's me Stacy, let us in."

A head appeared at the top window and peered down at us through the darkness.

"For the love of God, Liz, come down and let us in," Stacy screamed. "And hurry!"

"Hurry!" we screamed in chorus as we saw the guys' car turning the corner toward us.

Liz, bless her quick dear heart, was at the door almost immediately. We practically trampled over her to get inside that door. Wide-eyed and bewildered she led us to the sitting room, where we fell like dominoes into chairs and began recounting our tale. Liz looked out the window as if to confirm our story, and sure enough the car was parked outside, four guys sitting inside with no plans to move along.

"They're still out there," she informed us.

"Call the police," Mildred suggested.

"And tell them what?" Stacy cut her off. "They're all on the same side."

"She's right," Moira and Liz agreed. "They are all the same crowd up here."

Mildred and I, the two Southern idiots, didn't fully understand the fear of uniforms at work here. These girls had to take care of themselves by themselves.

"Ye'll have to spend the night," Liz announced.

Delighted with this invitation, we began to relax. One by one we reached up under our skirts, peeled off our torn, sweaty tights, and inspected our tired, sore feet. We were a sight! Liz pulled back the curtain, one more time, and peered out the window.

"They're still there," she continued apologetically. "Look girls, there's nothing they can do to you now. You're safe here till morning." She paused before adding, "Would ye mind awfully if I went back to bed? I've had a long day myself."

"Not at all," Stacy quipped. "You've just saved our lives. Go! We'll see you in the morning."

Reluctantly, Liz shuffled out the door and went back to her warm bed. One by one the rest of us fell asleep where we sat.

"They're gone," were the words of our alarm clock that morning. Mildred was up first and delighted to announce that we were free. The car was gone.

"That's all well and good," Stacy said, "but we'll have to go home a roundabout way just in case they're still lurking out there somewhere."

"Can't Liz drive us home?" I asked.

"Liz, doesn't own a car."

I had forgotten city dwellers rarely own cars.

"Let's just call a taxi. My feet are a mess," I complained.

No one contested this suggestion.

Not a word was spoken all the way back to the housing estate. Mildred and I gathered our things, thanked our hosts, and departed. I've not been back to Belfast since that trip. Moira and I lost touch over the years. I can't imagine why!

ENDLESS VISITORS

Over the course of my four years in Donegal, I had endless visitors. People tended to use me as a free "expert" tour guide to the North. I didn't mind. I was lonely in my Northern exile and welcomed anyone who'd consider a visit. Carmel, my younger sister, came North. She almost broke me out of house and home. My older sister came North. She couldn't understand why I "chose" to live in a war zone. Jerry came North and tried in vain to coax me out fishing along the banks of the River Finn. Margaret came North but didn't even notice she had changed locations. Orek, a Dutch friend of my older sister came North and couldn't take enough photographs.

Catherine was by far my most frequent, best loved, and tolerant houseguest.

Carmel, the judge and jury of my life, missed me so badly she couldn't wait to come see my foreign exile for herself. She was a tiresome houseguest, and I was glad to see the back of her and her endless complaining. Donegal, an Atlantic coastal county, is significantly further north, with a radically colder climate than inland Tipperary. It took a four-stone bag of coal a day to keep her fat backside toasted. She sat on that coal fire from morning to night and declined any offers to budge outside the door except to be taken to dinner. She insisted on being wined and dined at the best hotels and restaurants, refusing to drop her standard even in Donegal. Publically she ridiculed the locals and derided them for being so insular. Even I wasn't spared her contempt.

"I don't know how you can live in this God forsaken Arctic!"

"As if I had any choice in the matter!" I snapped back. "You have a short memory, my dear. This was the only place in Ireland desperate enough to have me."

Carmel had cried her eyes out when I left for Donegal, and now having seen how pathetic my life was, her pity turned to scorn. I felt an abject failure in her company.

Orek my sisters ex-boyfriend from Amsterdam, arrived uninvited on my doorstep. An expert on everything, he had all the answers and demanded a tour of the North to see what all the fuss was about.

"It's a war zone, isn't it? I've got to see this, get some pictures for my friends."

We spent Saturday in Derry. He toted that feckin' camera with him day and night, shooting at everything in sight. When an armored car stopped in front of us, he snapped. When a pair of fully armed soldiers passed on the street, he snapped again. When the police whirred through town in their reinforced cars, he snapped again. The shutters clipped all day long at micro speed. When we entered the Bogside and strolled around Freedom Wall, I begged him to put the camera away.

"This area is particularly sensitive to both sides," I explained. "They might think it's a gun."

"They'd never be that stupid!"

"People holding paint brushes have been shot dead. Please put the camera away. They will shoot you if they feel threatened," I warned.

"No, they won't," he protested stupidly. "I'm Dutch. King William and all that. The English love us. We're kinsmen."

"Like that's written across your chest! Don't Shoot. I'm Dutch!" I scoffed.

There was no dealing with his arrogance and stupidity. I couldn't wait to get him out of the North and out of my life.

In autumn, Teresa, my older sister, came home from Switzerland and decided to take advantage of my living so near the North to take a look for herself.

"Donegal is quaint and old-fashioned. A nice place to visit, but I couldn't live here," she confessed kindly.

Once we crossed the border, the tide turned, and she became quite strappy with me. I knew I needed to tip toe lightly around her or she would turn into a complete bitch and make shredded meat of me.

"What do you mean they might search us?" she asked when we pulled up to the border.

"They say we're going into a new country, so we have to be checked. They worry about guns and bombs and stuff like that."

"Switzerland is surrounded by many countries, and they never give me any hassle crossing in or out."

She wore me out with her stories of how perfectly peaceful her Swiss world was.

"Well, it's kinda different up here, though. You know, the whole question over who owns what."

She wasn't having any of it. I think she just wanted to be ornery. In town she became impatient because I circumnavigated the square trying to find a suitable parking spot.

"Why can't we park here? It's a perfectly good spot."

"It's a control zone. One of us will have to stay in the car if I park here."

"What do you mean I'll have to stay in the car? I want to go shopping too. You said yourself things are cheaper up here."

"Someone has to stay in the car. That's how it works. Then they know there isn't a bomb in it." It was frustrating trying to explain to her how the control zones worked, but she got it eventually, although she still complained bitterly about the stupidity of it all.

"Why do they carry so many guns?"

"For protection."

"What are those funny looking cars?"

"They're regular cars reinforced with bullet-proof glass and stuff."

"Why do they need all that protection?"

"Bombs, arrests, shoot outs and the likes. These things do happen and often," I assured her.

I was thankful for the silence that ensued, but knew she was taking time out to manufacture another complaint.

"So who drives the armored cars, and who drives the reinforced ones?"

"The army uses the armored cars, and the police use the reinforced ones. At least that's what I'm told."

"How do you know the good guys from the bad guys?"

"You don't."

A convoy of four armored cars roared through the main street as we sat in the car playing twenty questions.

"Where are all those trucks going in such a hurry?"

"I don't know. There must be trouble somewhere."

"So is that why they call it the troubles?"

"I don't know."

"You know very little for someone who lives here," she snarked.

I knew better than to respond. She was itching for a row, so she continued shooting questions at me like a rapidly firing Gatling gun.

"How come some have red berets and some have green ones?"

The questions went on and on. I was exhausted giving all the 'wrong answers!' Finally, after a whole day in the North, and much to my relief, she snapped. Her patience had run thin. She was done with the whole Northern Ireland thing.

"I want to go home. I'm tired of this place. It's like living in a war zone."

To make matters worse she added rather harshly, "I don't know what brought you up here in the first place. But then that's typical of you, isn't it? Always looking for attention."

The very next morning I drove her to the bus station and sent her back to her paradise.

Catherine was by far my most welcome visitor. Suddenly, out of nowhere and with great to-do, she'd roar up my driveway scattering gravel chips everywhere and slide to a scratching halt outside the front door.

"Kitty's here," she'd coo, announcing her arrival as she pushed in the hall door. My cold and lonely existence was set ablaze.

In the intervening months between her visits, I'd set my sights on some local hunk of gorgeousness. Carefully laid plans to ensnare my prey would be working brilliantly. Then Catherine would arrive. Together we'd scour the local bars until we found the one where my target was innocently leaning into the bar and enjoying a quiet drink. Over the course of the evening, friends, suitors, and hangers-on joined the two of us. Usually Catherine entertained the lot, allowing me the freedom to admire my target from a distance and contemplate my next move. Unfortunately, Catherine was my best friend in the whole world, and eventually she tricked or coerced me into confiding my latest crush.

"Don't worry, Gabrielle," she answered again and again, "I'll get him for you." And off she'd go, straight to my heartthrob, determined to get him for me. Without fail, each and every conquest of this kind resulted in the guy falling head over heels in love with Catherine, and I remained the gooseberry in the booth.

I loved visitors, but when they departed I was left behind feeling more alienated from my previous life than ever. A hollowed, carved-out feeling in my gut gave testimony to the fact that I was a disemboweled entity; my heart was far south, but my body was in Donegal. When Catherine left, the pain was worst. For a week after her departure, I'd listen to Paul Young's "Every Time You Go Away" and cry my eyes out.

Gabrielle Ní Mheachair

BREAK IN

After our trip to Belfast, our fascination for men in uniform, guns, and graffiti waned considerably. We tried to adjust to ordinary life, but it was difficult. Normal society challenged us daily, and when Catherine came to visit, there was no stopping us. We became "girls gone wild." The Donegal locals looked on as if they were watching a two-man circus show. They were not prepared for the likes of us. We shocked them into the next century. The whole town seemed to come out to stare when Catherine came North. She took full advantage of her surroundings, her anonymity, and me, to go stark, raving mad. The tales of her visits are probably nightly toasts in Ballybofey, Stanorlar, and Letterkenny. I can see them now, all gathered around the fireplace in the Ballyraine Hotel asking, "Whatever happened to the two girls from Tipperary?"

When Catherine got bored with her life in Cork City, she came to visit me in Donegal. We lived the high life, eating dinner at hotels and frequenting discos, bars, and late-night parties. Sometimes we went to visit Mildred in Carndonagh, though I regularly balked at taking her there for fear she would ruin my relationship with Mildred, which was not beyond the realm of possibility the way Catherine carried on. However, there was one weekend I relented, and we arrived on Mildred's doorstep only to find the place empty. Not a soul in sight!

"Now, what?" asked Catherine.

"Don't know. But I'm not driving all the way back to Ballybofey tonight."

"Let's check for a key."

We walked all around the house, searching under mats, flowerpots, large stones, tin cans, and anything remotely likely to conceal a key. No luck!

"What about the windows or the doors? There might be one open," Catherine suggested.

Again we circled the house and were delighted to find the bathroom window open. It was a tall, skinny, opaque window with an open-out section at the top. A long, black, metal notched arm held this part slightly ajar, but it was very high up and the opening seemed way too small for an adult body to get through.

"There's no way in hell we'll reach that high," I said.

"Sure we will," the ever-optimistic Catherine responded. "If you give me a leg up, I can reach the ledge and pull myself up the rest of the way."

"You'll never fit through the window. It's too small."

"Just give me a leg up," she demanded.

So I did.

Catherine pulled herself upward till she was able to stand on the protruding windowsill. Then I pushed her legs up behind her as she wiggled her body head first through the window and down onto the toilet cistern. At one point, a neighbor came out her back door carrying a basket of laundry. She marched over to her clothesline, which stretched from one end of the yard to the other. Beginning at the farthest point, she carefully shook out each item of clothing before skillfully hanging it up to dry in the crisp cold wind. She worked her way, shirt by shirt, to the opposite end, which was just outside our fence. When she turned around to go back inside, she spotted the pair of us. The lower half of Catherine's body was still hanging out the window, and I was struggling to heave it upward. I turned and smiled, nodding, "How ya, misses! Lovely evening isn't it?" and returned to gently easing the last of the body through the open window.

The neighbor scowled at me before rushing back inside.

"Who's that?" Catherine asked.

"It's the neighbor. She's not very friendly. I don't know what her problem is. Maybe she doesn't like renters living next door. It lowers the value of her property."

"Never mind that now, just keep shoving, I'm almost down."

It was no time at all before Catherine successfully strutted out the back door and let me in. Immediately she set about rummaging through the cupboards and found all the ingredients she needed to bake. Donning an apron, she lit the oven and began baking scones and an apple tart.

"I'll light the fire."

Fortunately there was an ample supply of coal and turf out back, and in no time at all I had a roaring fire going. The house warmed up nicely. Catherine put an apple tart in the oven, set the timer, and went outside for a cigarette. I set the table for tea and began washing Mildred's breakfast dishes and Catherine's baking implements. The timer beeped. Catherine took out the tart and shoved in a batch of scones.

"Lord that's great now, fresh apple tart and tea. I'm starving," she announced. "You make the tea, I'll cut the tart. I baked. I get the first slice."

There was no argument there. Besides, there was more than enough tart for both of us.

We were just about to sit down to eat when the doorbell rang. My heart leapt for joy.

"Mildred's home, and just in time for tea and tart."

I raced to the door only to find two tall, very serious Gardaí staring accusingly at me.

"Can I help you?" I asked as nicely as possible.

"The neighbors called in saying they saw someone break in. Have you seen or heard anything suspicious?"

"Nothing at all. Of course we're not long home."

"Do you mind if we take a look around?"

"Be my guest."

I opened the door wide to let them inside.

"How are ya?" said Catherine as she sat herself down to snatch the first slice of tart while it was still steamy-moist and hot.

"Would you like a slice?" she spluttered through her stuffed mouth.

"No thanks, ma'am, we're on duty."

"Suit yourselves," she muttered, disappointed.

They smiled at her and continued to potter about the kitchen, looking at the window latches and door locks.

"Everything looks in order."

"Do you mind if we go into the bedrooms?"

"Not at all, not at all."

They searched every room in the house, then returned to the kitchen.

"Well?" I asked.

"Everything is in order. There's no sign of a disturbance. That bathroom window is open, right enough, but 'tis too narrow for anyone to get in."

"Oh, yea, t'would be right enough. 'Tis terribly narrow," grinned Catherine.

"And ye heard nothing and saw nothing?"

"Not a thing. But like I said, we're only just in before ye."

"Would you like some apple tart before ye go?" Catherine coaxed again.

What is she thinking? We've got to get rid of them. I glared at a flippant Catherine, hoping she'd get the hint.

"No, thank you, ma'am."

Relieved at their refusal, I wedged my body between her and the pair, escorting them out the door as quickly as I could.

"Goodnight lads, and thanks very much."

With my back to the door, I paused for breath, then returned to the kitchen with a broad grin slapped across my face. I was thankful that both Gardaí were middle-aged, married, and not hungry. The outcome of the incident would have been considerably different had they been young, free, single, and hungry.

When Mildred returned home some hours later, she was surprised to find a clean house, a blazing fire, a hot apple tart, and brown bread scones all waiting for her. She could hardly be mad at us!

KNEECAPPING

When Catherine set her mind to something, nothing or no one could stop her. While this was a lot of fun, most of the time it had serious and unexpected repercussions. Crossing the border with her proved to be quite the adventure. She hit on the Gardaí on the Irish side and the RUC on the other. She arranged dates, having no plans to ever show up. However, that was before George. He was a tall, dark, handsome fellow with a sculpted body and irresistible charm. He looked like the movie star Liam Neeson.

We pulled up close to the guardrail at the border crossing and parked, waiting for someone to come out of the barracks and check our IDs. It seemed like ages before this hunk of an RUC man loped lazily toward us. He was finishing a snack and chewed with a grin as he approached us in the car. Catherine rolled down the passenger window and leaned out to flirt outrageously with him. He was so taken by her charm and pretty face that he walked around to her side of the car and inspected my documents through her window. I sat there, waiting patiently as she led him up the usual garden path and made arrangements for a date she had no intention of keeping.

Some weeks later, after Catherine had returned to Cork City, I was sitting at our local pub surrounded by friends passing the night away when a stranger sat down beside me. I assumed he was an acquaintance of one of the group. so I engaged his polite conversation. When the music got particularly loud, he leaned in close to me and whispered, "I have a message for you."

"A message for me, from who?"

"Just listen to the message," he urged. "*If you continue to fraternize with the RUC, you will be kneecapped.*"

"What!" I exclaimed aloud.

Without further ado, the stranger rose to his feet, politely excused himself from our company, and vanished into the dancing crowd. I was paralyzed with shock.

Everyone stared at me. They all had the same question on their lips.

"Who was that?"

"I don't know."

"Oh come on, he sat beside you."

"I thought one of you knew him."

"Nope!"

"What did he want?"

"I've no idea."

"Well what did he say to you?"

"Nothing."

"He must have said something, You look really upset."

"I couldn't hear him. The music is too loud."

"Ah, come on, something just happened."

"I said nothing happened, and that's the end of it."

Friends and family who know me well are aware that it is not wise to push me when I get to that level of irritability. As Mother would say, "Let sleeping dogs lie." This petite little girl has mighty force when push comes to shove. Thankfully, my friends were well aware of my ornery disposition and let it be.

I sank back into the leather seat in silent disbelief. My mind was buzzing, trying to comprehend what had just happened. I ran his words through my brain a hundred times trying to decipher what it meant, *"If you continue to fraternize with the RUC, you will be kneecapped."*

What on Earth was he talking about? I knew without a shard of a doubt that I was the last person on the planet who could ever be accused of fraternizing with the RUC. His message made no sense. Noticing my unusually subdued and distracted demeanor my friends began shooting more questions at me. They wanted answers.

"So who was that, really?"

"I said I don't know, and I don't know. I've had a long day. I think I'll make it an early night."

Abruptly, I jumped to my feet, excused myself, and left. I knew they would talk about me when I was gone, but I couldn't care less about that. I was quite shaken and very upset. A complete stranger had just threatened me, and for no apparent reason, at least none I could figure out.

The minute I got in the door at home I called my friend, Josh, and recounted what had happened.

"Josh, I was just told that I was going to be kneecapped!" I exclaimed.

"I know," he responded calmly.

"What! How could you know? It just happened."

"You're being watched. I warned you to stay out of the North, but there's no talking to you, Gabrielle. You won't listen to anyone."

"Why am I being watched, Josh?" I begged, hoping for an answer that made sense.

"Well," he dragged it out, "it seems your car has been spotted outside the RUC bar in Strabane."

"I have never in my life been in a bar in Strabane. I don't even know one bar from another, let alone which one the RUC drink at," I snapped angrily.

"Well you can't miss the RUC one," he said. "It's right at the top of town on the road to Derry. It's all barricaded in galvanized sheets to prevent it from being burned down or bombed out."

"Actually, I remember seeing that place on my way to Derry. I had no idea it was a bar, let alone an RUC bar," I confessed.

"That's where the RUC socialize," he repeated. "That's the one where your car was spotted recently."

"You know very well, Josh, that I wouldn't step inside an RUC bar if it meant saving my life. I was never in that place."

"Well your car was parked outside it. More than once!" he added for emphasis.

"More than once? You've got to be kidding me! Is someone trying to set me up?"

Suddenly it dawned on me.

"Catherine! It was Catherine. I bet she met the hunk from the border while I was at school! I left her my car while I was working so she could run around and shop."

"Well, they don't care who's driving. It's you they've fingered, and if I were you I wouldn't be crossing that border anytime soon in that little car of yours."

"Great!" I exclaimed. "Am I to be a prisoner in my own country now?"

"Maybe this'll teach you to listen to those who know what they are talking about," Josh added.

"How am I going to stop them from kneecapping me? Will they still come after me?" I worried aloud half-hoping Josh had connections.

"You'll be fine if you stay out of the firing line," he assured me.

Needless to say, I was seriously alarmed and avoided the North for a very long time thereafter. I was not about to risk my lovely legs! As for Catherine, she was never getting behind the wheel of my car again!

Gabrielle Ní Mheachair

FINE BODIES

"You'll never find a man with that attitude of yours," my mother complained regularly. And she was right. I couldn't get a man for the life of me, and it was, "that attitude of mine." I wasn't short of men in my life. It's just that they were either the wrong type, married, divorced, too serious, too flip, unrequited, more interested in drink than me, or one-night stands who never wanted to see me again. Plus, I was easily bored, finding that faraway fields did indeed look greener. I wanted it all: the bird in the bush and one in each hand. One can hardly blame a hungry child for sampling all the dishes!

I moved to Donegal with a man in my life, Paul, the man who had gotten the site from his grandmother. He wanted to build a house, get married, settle down, have children, all noble ideas, but I was in the flower of my youth and those things were abhorrent to me. When my high school friends were being picked up, dumped, dated, groped, courted—whatever—I was a caged bird. At twenty-one I graduated college and the cage door flung open. I flew out ready to see and conquer that unknown world of men. Fortunately, for me, my sister—a year younger—was right there beside me with the same appetite for adventure and men. We were, truth be told, man mad.

Paul was a lovely man, and I was in love with him, in my own way. He was willing to wait for me to get this madness out of my system. Bless his darling heart! But one day having driven from Cork to Donegal, the poor lad was greeted at my door like a stranger. I had completely fallen out of love with him. It was as instant as that. The morning he called to say he was coming, I was in love with him and dreamt of his arrival all day long. That same evening, when he arrived on the threshold, I had nothing to offer. It was all gone, poof, out the door, dissipating into the clouds settled over the River Finn across the road.

This abrupt inexplicable alteration in my feelings terrified me. I kept rehearsing the question, *What if I get married and wake up one morning totally out of love? What do I do then?* The possibility haunted me. This momentous revelation colored my view of love, and from that day forward I was in no hurry to commit to anyone. This experience cemented my "attitude." Poor Paul was devastated. Everyone chided me for letting a good man go. There was no explaining what happened, what went wrong, or whose fault it was. I had nothing for them. Hot one day, cold the next! That was the extent of it. Paul was a firmly closed book, and that was that. But I still got it in the ear every time I went home, from everyone who knew him, for years! With Paul gone, I was free to tackle all the men of Donegal, Ireland, or the world! I rallied, got bored, and dumped, or I rallied, was used for a one-night snoggle, and dumped. More often the latter!

The border between Northern and Southern Ireland was secured by the finest bodies in all of Ireland: young, newly recruited Gardaí. Acceptance into the Templemore Garda College, the hub of my hometown, was exceptionally competitive. There were very high standards for height, body weight, and fitness level. Most were six-foot tall, handsome, clean cut, with superbly toned, muscular bodies. Graduating Gardaí were at their peak. Having grown up a mile from the training center, these fine specimens of men left us in no doubt as to what a man should look like. Much to our father's disgust, we judged and categorized all men according to the quality of their "fine bodies." When choosing a man there was only one question worth asking, "Is he a fine body?"

Donegal had an abundance of fine bodies. It seemed the finest and the fittest Gardaí recruits were drafted for border duty right after graduation. We were determined to sample the lot. It was exhausting work, prying those men away from the bar where they drowned their misery nightly. They hated border duty and were just putting in time till they were transferred back South to their mammies or their local steady girlfriends. Our interaction with them was a commensurate affair. The boundaries were clear; we toyed with them and they with us.

Local boys were different. They were looking for a good time en route to a wife. Their movements were monitored, manipulated, and approved by parents and friends. These lads were under the microscope of the small insular society in which they lived, a concept I failed to grasp.

My friend group fancied Brennan, but he asked me out. I was chuffed. Being members of the local drama club, we decided to see the latest show. At intermission Brennan excused himself and went to the bathroom. He never came back. I was indignant. Rather than leave a really good show, I moved way up into the corner of the back row as far as possible from our previous seats. Sometime before the end of the play, Brennan returned to an empty seat. I was tickled pink watching him become ill at ease and his neck strain as he searched the dark theater for his date. After the show I left through the emergency doors, leaving him standing like an eejit at the main door. Later he explained that he was snatched from the bathroom to man the concession stand. "Too bad," I said. "I wait for no man." That was the end of that.

Next came Noah, the hunk on crutches. Catherine abandoned me at the Beehive Club one Wednesday night for an incredibly tall, blond, handsome Garda. Once again, I found myself a spare wheel in an overcrowded disco hall, alone and embarrassed, sipping my soda and lime, hoping no friends witnessed my dismal state. There was nothing to do but talent-spot.

A solitary pathetic-looking lad caught my eye on the opposite side of the dance floor. He was lolling against a bar stool in an uncomfortable pose, his right leg imprisoned inside a knee-high plaster-of-Paris cast. A pair of wooden crutches lay propped by his side. A quick body scan reported a perfect specimen: tall, toned body; black hair; unusually green eyes; short-cropped hair; one stud diamond earring; and a lonely pout on perfectly kissable lips. It was my duty to cheer him up.

Noah was only too happy to share his rugby tragedy. Captivated by his woeful tale and sheer physical masculinity, I was smitten. This hunk of gorgeousness was so interesting, nonthreatening, casual, and fun to be with that time flew by. Too soon the barman began yelling, "Time, gentlemen please, time. Finish up now. The bar is closed." Shortly thereafter he set about ejecting the clientele, at which point Noah cleverly begged a ride home. Of course he had no idea I had a sister in tow.

My heart went out to the poor lad, because he had to sit in the rear with his foot across the backseat and endure Catherine's rude harassment the whole way home. Though much to his credit, he was well able for her, and we ended up parked outside his gate the pair of them verbally sparring for another ten minutes.

"Guys, I have work in the morning."

"So do I," he responded.

"Well get out then. I like my bed even if you don't."

He awkwardly struggled to pull his disabled body out

of the car and hobbled directly to the gate before turning to wave goodnight. I didn't expect he would ever want to see the pair of us again.

Low and behold, a week later I ran into him on the street as he dragged himself crutch by crutch up the hill toward his home.

"Hey, Noah, how's the leg?" I asked in my friendliest tone.

"Grand," he said, showing his bright white teeth and perfect smile.

Well at least he's not mad at me, I thought. It seemed to me he had enough sense to distinguish between the two sisters. Few ever do. We're always painted with the same brush! I have to admire a man who can see us as individuals. Usually that's one of the standards by which I judged all men: Can he resist Catherine, and can he tell us apart ?Maybe this was an intelligent one after all!

"Have you long more in the cast?"

"Dunno. Hey, any chance of a lift home?" he boldly asked.

"Sure, I'm parked just outside the bank. Wait for me there. I'll be back in a tick."

Noah and I became an item. We met after work each day and took joint pleasure in attending movies, folk nights, and dances, and when the cast was removed, we took long walks in the forest. Unfortunately, the local social police were outraged. He was regularly hassled for dating an older woman. I was harangued for dating a younger man.

A trip to Carndonagh was speedily arranged. I needed to consult with my coolly sensible, brutally honest friend Mildred. Much to my utter indignation and vehement counter-arguments, she was determined to concur with the locals. Upon my return, I shared my concern with Noah. He was passionately against ending the relationship, as was I. However, the relentless persecution became intolerable. Reluctantly, I cut the cord. To my sheer devastation Noah walked straight from my arms into the loving bosom of an even older woman, but she was local. Different rules applied.

Hot on the heels of Noah came Finn. He too was a younger man, giving testimony to my own immaturity. We laughed, danced, dined at fine hotels, and watched movies, until once again the social police interfered. Spooked by his friends' opinions, he disappeared from my life as quickly as he had dashed in.

Oisín stood in the wings and shadows watching and waiting for the opportunity to spring. I noticed him there but gave no encouragement. There were finer men to lure into my net. Though kind and sweet, he was short, so he failed the "fine body" standard. However, it was only a matter of time before he pounced, pushing all others aside and demanding my undivided attention. A man of the world, the silver-tongued Oisín was surprisingly seductive. My ego was all ears.

Being the owner of a four-star hotel on the west coast of Ireland may not have compensated for his lack of height, but it was most alluring. Irresistible visions of sitting in a plushy decorated lounge, sipping white wine, and nibbling on freshly caught salmon with pampering waiters meeting my every need convinced me to visit. A date was agreed upon, and on the following Friday, after a long day at school, I drove toward the west coast of Ireland.

My excursion snaked through bare, rounded mountains and narrow river valleys. It was a beautiful trip. The hillsides were covered in purple heather and yellow gorse. Here and there little chocolate squares were cleared to harvest the dark-brown turf. Tiny two-room cottages grew on precarious sites, preserving the sparse, fertile scraps for cultivation. Fluffy, yellow-blond sheep littered the slopes, grazing on rare sprigs of juicy grass. I drove and drove until there was no road left, just the pounding Atlantic roaring straight for me.

Following the sign for the hotel, I turned left, then took another left into a wide tarmac road that led to a long, rectangular, flat, black-roofed, white-walled hotel that spoiled the natural beauty of the ruggedly rural coastline. I was utterly disappointed. This was a far cry from the anticipated gray manor home nestled among ancient oaks at the end of a long, winding gravel driveway. I sat in the car contemplating my next move. Do I turn around and go home or take advantage of a free hotel night?

Obviously expected, the receptionist led me to my room and offered tea in the lounge after I had unpacked and settled in. Not bad, I thought. My suite was huge, with a large king-size bed and a TV, all for little old me. I jumped on the bed and began rolling around testing the mattress when a loud distinctive knock brought me to my senses. It had to be Oisín. He welcomed me with a friendly hug.

"Well, do you like your room?"

"It's huge. I love the TV and the bed."

He walked over to the window and beckoned me to join him there. Swishing back the curtains he declared, "Have you ever seen a view quite like that?"

The waves bashed violently against the cliffs, and the sea spray formed little rainbows all along the coastline. It was enchanting. (*Not romantic*, I reminded myself).

He went on to give me a history of the place and his dreams for the future of this hotel. I responded appropriately in all the right places, challenged to sound casual, and uncommitted.

"Would you like a cuppa?"

"Yes, I'd kill for a decent cup of tea. It had been a long, tedious trek across the mountains. Oh, and I want chocolate biscuits as well. A Cadbury's snack would do; the yellow ones, not the pink."

"You are demanding," he grinned. "But I like a woman who speaks her mind and knows what she wants."

He led me to the lounge where he set me up with tea and chocolate biscuits.

"I have some work to finish up. Will you be OK on your own till dinnertime?" he apologized.

Naturally I went for the salmon and white wine; someone else was paying! After a long, interesting dinner we toured the hotel and ended up in the private lounge watching *Top Gun*. The steamy love scenes made me anxious that Oisín might be getting ideas! When he suggested we take a drive out the peninsula to Maghery, I jumped to my feet and practically ran for the door.

"This is the most westerly pub in Ireland," Oisín claimed. "I come here to get away from it all."

Sure enough, the pub was filled with friends and welcoming locals who invited us to join their games of darts and cards, singing, dancing, and political arguments. It was the wee hours of the morning by the time we returned to the hotel, where I didn't sleep a wink, worrying that Oisín might sneak into my suite. After all, he had master keys to all the rooms!

I should have been ashamed of myself for thinking so ill of him, and he nothing but a gentleman from start to finish. Darling Oisín could have been my best friend. He was a very fine man, but not my type and obviously already conquered. Men were a conquest; once captured I cast them aside, and moved on to the next challenge. Mother would have cried big salty tears at the opportunities I let slip. Thankfully, her absolute ignorance was my bliss.

THE NEWSPAPER MAN

Donegal provided an assortment of victories and failures, but the most remarkable was the newspaperman. Spring arrived and the weather in Donegal was picking up, offering nice, crisp weather that would skin the hide off a lesser being, but was delightfully cool for those of us who had survived the winter. Not only had spring come, but the sun came shining through my life and would last for seven whole days! Catherine had a week off and decided to spend it with me. Her arrival brightened my dreary life.

"Where are we for tonight?" she asked expectantly.

"No idea. What do you have in mind?"

"Let's get dinner at the hotel and hang out there for a while."

A five-course meal served over several hours was just what the doctor ordered after a grueling day at school.

Catherine filled the deep tub with hot water and soaked in it for an hour. By the time she was done topping up her bath with hot water, there was naught but a lukewarm dribble left for my quick shower. We dressed in our finery, completing the process with makeup and hair spray. Catherine looked gorgeous. I was a good second.

I drove and kept the keys. Experience had taught me I didn't want to be stranded when Catherine absconded with some fine hunk.

Thankfully, dinner was superb and held its own against Catherine's fancy, Cork City joints. Larson's Hotel never failed to serve the best homegrown, local produce and the finest Irish salmon ever tasted. After hours of relaxed eating, we retired to the lounge for drinks and sat in a cozy, secluded alcove facing the bar. The place was empty save for a well-dressed gentleman sipping on a whiskey hiding behind the *Irish Independent*.

"There'll be no action here tonight," I assured Catherine. "It's Monday."

"Let's head for Letterkenny then," she suggested. "There's bound to be more action there."

"It's a school night. I'd rather go home. We've loads of time for Letterkenny. You're here for the week."

As we finished our drinks, a tall, blond stranger walked into the bar and slid onto a barstool at the counter. He ordered quickly. While he waited for his drink, he surveyed the room as if searching for someone.

"Cor, he's a hunk," Catherine whispered excitedly.

"He's not local. He must be a salesman."

"Who cares?" Catherine spat.

"Salesmen have awful reputations. Best not mess with him." I counseled.

Catherine never heeded my advice. In fact, it seems, she was determined to do the exact opposite. Pulling herself upright out of her comfy seat, she cupped her breasts and thrust them upward to form deep cleavage. Then she waddled sexily toward the bar, shoving right up beside the blond salesman using her classic opening line, "Hiiiiii," all the while batting her eyelids and smiling lustily. It was embarrassing to watch her in action. There she was, my sister, again and again toying with men's affections only to walk out the door when she got bored or tired. Few of them ever saw it coming. Many didn't care. They enjoyed the game. Others got irritated, some became angry, and one or two got violent.

Here we go again, I thought, as I sat there a lonely gooseberry in an almost empty lounge. I dreaded the arrival of the locals and the ensuing humiliation of being found sitting alone in a bar on a Monday night. It was then I spotted a movement from the corner of my eye. It was the newspaperman shifting in his seat. He neatly folded his newspaper and put it on the table. I could tell he was distracted by the flirtatious behavior of the two at the bar. I made a trip to the bathroom and deliberately returned through a door situated directly behind him. He was sipping his drink, amused by the banter between Catherine and the salesman. I brushed alongside him and asked, "Are you finished with your newspaper, sir?"

"As a matter of fact I am," he said in a very educated tone that reminded me of my father.

"Would you mind if I borrowed it?" I went on.

"Of course not. It's all yours," he said kindly, as he picked it up, folded it into a long narrow wad, and handed it to me.

"Thank you."

I turned on my heels, returned to my nook, and hid behind the newspaper for the remainder of the evening.

After what felt like hours, I spotted Catherine heading for the bathroom. She gave me "the look" as she turned the corner. I promptly followed, using the quick route—the door behind the newspaperman. He smiled at me, and I could tell he made the connection between us girls for the first time. I smiled back.

In the bathroom Catherine announced, "We need to leave now."

I knew the routine. The guy had come on strong. She was having none of it. The game had gotten sour. It was rescue time. She returned to the bar with me following at a polite distance. The newspaperman was gone. I walked to the counter and very snippily declared, "Catherine, we need to leave now. I have work in the morning." She feigned a protest. He offered to take her home and relieve me of my chore. I refused. I got snippier. She grabbed her bag and marched out the door without as much as a look back.

"Where too now?" she asked.

"We're going home," I insisted. "I've had enough for one night. Besides, I have an early start."

She didn't argue.

For the rest of the week we hung out with friends at various local bars and clubs. However, we both agreed that on Friday we were going to visit Mildred in Carndonagh to watch the Eurovision Song Contest with her friends.

"Let's do dinner at the Ballybay Hotel on our way," Catherine suggested.

Friday didn't come half-fast enough. I hadn't seen my dear friend, Mildred, since early winter. After school I changed into nice, casual driving gear and together Catherine and I headed for Letterkenny and the Ballybay Hotel for dinner. Neither of us had eaten there before, and we arrived too early for serving.

"What now?" Catherine asked.

Having learned from our previous breaking-and-entering escapade that Mildred didn't get home until after six on Fridays, I was in no great hurry to Carndonagh.

"Let's just hang around until serving time," I suggested. I really wanted to have a fancy hotel dinner, and it was Catherine's turn to pay.

The Ballybay Hotel was probably the largest and most modern hotel on the Inis Eogain peninsula. It lacked the dark carved wood finishes, stuffed couches, and fireplaces of older hotels. I dislike the modern smooth lines, large windows, blond wood, silver chrome and brushed-nickel finishes with gas fires or radiators. Clean angular colorless designs aggravated my sense of cold and loneliness.

"Surely they have a cozy lounge for residents," I suggested.

We explored behind doors until we found the private residence lounge. As expected, it was a mite cozier than the bar and the reception area. Boldly we marched inside and ordered our usual, lemon and lime with ice. Then we retired to a corner where we had full view of our surroundings.

There was a man sitting with his back to the window reading a newspaper. It was hard to make him out because the light was bad at that angle. Two men leaned across the bar discussing the Gaelic Athletic Association (GAA) with the barman. Their conversation was getting quite heated. Obviously they disagreed over something. Their banter reminded me of my uncles, who were avid GAA fans, arguing with my father, who thought them all a bunch of uneducated hooligans looking for an excuse to wallop each other with hurleys. After about thirty minutes Catherine began to get restless. There was no action for her here, and eavesdropping on other people's conversations wasn't her thing.

"I'm bored," she complained. "Let's just go."

"But I want dinner."

"We can stop somewhere else on the way."

"I was really looking forward to sampling the menu here," I whined. Besides, I knew this was the last restaurant open from here to Carndonagh.

"We can come back next time I'm up. At least now we know the times."

"Fine."

We were draining our glasses when two men strolled into the bar and positioned themselves in our direct line of vision. Their intentions were obvious. I didn't like the look of either one of them, but Catherine wasn't one to miss an opportunity to flirt. She decided to order new drinks. Off she swaggered, straight to the bar, and sandwiched her slim form between the new arrivals. The men were amused. As per usual she was onstage and the entertainment began. The barman put her drinks on the counter. One of the guys insisted on paying. Catherine was delighted. My drink was never delivered, and the ice turned to water as it sat on the bar waiting to be claimed. There wasn't a chance in hell I was going to pick it up or join her game. No way was I going to be beholden to either of those men. Besides, I was needed to bring up the rear when it was time to flee. Shortly thereafter one of the men excused himself and left. Now Catherine had the one she wanted all to herself, and unsurprisingly I was the spare wheel in the corner. There was only one thing for it. I needed reading material.

With great difficulty I summoned the courage to walk across the room toward the gentleman in the window seat who was still reading his newspaper.

"Excuse me, sir," I whispered. Then pointing to the fold of newspaper on the table, I continued, "Are you finished with that part of the paper?" He slowly lowered the newspaper, looked me squarely in the eyes, and asked, "Do you make a habit of asking strange men in bars for their newspapers?"

Imagine my disconcertion when I discovered that this was the same newspaperman from the hotel on Monday. My face flushed red. My ears burned. My mouth went dry. In fact I was so embarrassed, I struggled to stall the tears mounting toward my eyes. Being a thorough gentleman he recognized my predicament and invited me to sit down.

"Why don't you have a seat?" he said, pointing to the comfy chair beside him.

Without thinking I collapsed onto the nearest stool, which was directly across the table from him.

"Do you really want the newspaper?"

"What do you mean?"

He nodded in the direction of Catherine and asked, "Your friend?"

"My sister."

"You're kidding," he joked.

"No really, she's my sister. I take after Dad's side of the family, the dark Mahers, and she takes after the tall, blond, blue-eyed Ryans of Mother's side."

His casual chatter was relaxing, and I was truly disappointed when the dinner bell disrupted our conversation.

"That's the dinner bell. We're having dinner here, or at least that was the plan," I told him.

"You're welcome to join me if your sister has other plans," he offered.

"I don't know if I can do that. She might need me."

"Why don't you ask her?"

Catherine was so busy with her own conquest she failed to notice I had changed seats and found company of my own. I politely interrupted her and asked her if she was interested in a free dinner. She cast an almost disinterested glance in the direction of my newspaperman.

"He's gorgeous," she spluttered brazenly in front of the other guy.

"He's offering to buy us dinner."

"Let's go then," she announced jumping off the bar stool and abandoning her love interest without as much as a good-bye or see ya later.

She swaggered shamelessly toward the newspaperman smiling all the way. He suppressed a grin.

"Hi, I'm Catherine," she whispered seductively.

"Please to meet you," he responded politely. "I'm David. Would you care to join us," he added, gesturing to the seat across the table from him.

"It's so nice of you to invite us to dinner," she schmoozed.

"I don't mind at all. I was planning on having dinner here myself. We might as well team up, and of course, it's my treat. I'm delighted to have such beautiful company."

Catherine slid into the seat closest to him and began chatting in her usual beguiling manner. He appeared amused and leaned back into his chair, rested his elbow on the armrest, and threw his right leg up over his left leg, making it clear he was giving her his full attention. She was intent on conquering this man too.

He was attractive. His body was splendid, tall, slim, broad-shouldered, and immaculately dressed. The absence of a ring indicated he was unmarried. His eyes appeared to be smiling, though I perceived a hint of deep pain inside those dark-brown pools. A sprinkling of acne scars gave him a rugged look. His thick brown hair was well groomed, and his warm smile was trimmed with gleaming white teeth. This man was a long way from the farm. He was obviously well educated, well traveled, and well heeled. None of this was lost on Catherine.

Dinner took ages. I became a anxious about the time. We still had an hour and a half to our final destination. I worried Mildred would be irritated if we arrived at all hours. But a free, sumptuous meal was not to be rushed.

"What about a cocktail after dinner?" David offered. There was no way we were dallying for cocktails.

"We'd love to, but we're expected in Carndonagh tonight."

"That's a shame. What about same time, same place tomorrow night?" he suggested out of the blue.

"What?" I almost shouted in disbelief.

"Well, you ladies are such fine company. Why not meet me here tomorrow night, and we can do cocktails or another dinner if you wish?"

My head spun. What is wrong with this man?

"That a great idea!" Catherine interjected.

"No, it is not," I fought back.

"Why not?"

"We're spending the weekend with Mildred, and that's that."

"Fine then," said a pouty Catherine, "You spend the weekend with Mildred, and I'll come to dinner. She's your friend, not mine."

"You're not taking my car."

"Ladies, I hate to interrupt, but why don't you bring Mildred with you?"

At this point I was getting highly irritated with Catherine and had no reservations about completely losing my cool in public.

"Look," I insisted in a firm, unbending tone, "a whole gang of us is watching the Eurovision Song Contest at one of the teacher's houses tomorrow night, and I'm not missing it."

"How about you invite them all to watch the Eurovision contest here on the big screen TV? You can invite the whole town if you like."

Catherine whined and pouted. I relented.

"I'll ask to see who's interested, and if Mildred is willing to come, we'll come, but I'll not come without her."

"That's settled then," he said with a broad grin and jumped to his feet. "Tomorrow night at six, right here."

We thanked him for the meal, shook hands, and left.

All the way to Carndonagh, Catherine ranted and raved about how gorgeous David was. He was every woman's dream, handsome, rich, generous, and intelligent.

"Don't you think he's a hunk?" she asked looking for affirmation.

"Yea, he's good looking and seems to be quite the gentleman, but he's not my type. He's too old. He must be at least thirty."

"I like mature men. They know how to treat a woman, and thirty's not old."

Thus went the conversation the whole trip.

Mildred was obviously anxious when we arrived. She had expected us earlier. We were only delighted to tell her the reason we were delayed. She laughed heartily at my misfortune to be caught in the same predicament twice.

"What are the odds of you hitting on the same man twice in one week? Only you, Gabrielle," she snickered. "These kinds of things only ever happen to you."

"Well, what do you want to do about tomorrow night?" I asked when the laughter died down.

"Of course I'm going," Mildred replied. "I wouldn't miss it for the world. I simply must see this newspaperman for myself. He sounds fascinating."

Then she turned to Catherine and added, "He must be very taken by you to be willing to invite the whole town."

Smiling smugly, Catherine stretched across the couch in front of the TV, content in the knowledge we were meeting her newest admirer tomorrow night.

Saturday afternoon I was clock watching and growing ever more impatient waiting for Catherine to get ready. Time was slipping away, and we needed to get going.

"One would think she was going to a ball!" I complained.

Mildred and I had made no such effort. Jeans and a T-shirt were just fine.

"Would you hurry up," I yelled down the hallway. "We'll miss the opening ceremonies."

"I'm coming, I'm coming," she replied for the fifth time.

Finally, hobbling on one high heel with the other in hand, she joined us at the door.

"About time," I snapped.

At breakneck speed we arrived in Letterkenny with time to spare. But when we got to the hotel, there was no one there to greet us. I had this sinking feeling in the pit of my stomach that we had been stood up. My mind buzzed through possible scenarios as to where we should go from there. Then out of the dark shadows our host appeared. He too was all dressed up. He wore a deep-blue, crisply pressed woolen suit; a white shirt; and a contrasting red patterned tie. He cast a striking pose as he sauntered toward us with a broad grin across his face. I almost gasped. For the first time since we had met him, I was truly impressed.

Now I know what Catherine sees in him, I confessed to myself. *He is gorgeous.*

I sneaked a look at Mildred, and she gave me an approving smile.

"Not bad," she whispered.

"Ladies," he announced, "would you like to follow me?"

Suddenly I felt under dressed. He was treating us like celebrities, even though Mildred and I looked scruffy and out of place. Catherine walked shoulder to shoulder with David, as Mildred and I brought up the rear. We found ourselves in a private room all arranged just for us. A big screen TV sat facing several armchairs, a couch, and a coffee table laden with snacks.

"This is like a luxury living room," Catherine ex-claimed as she linked arms with David and practically dragged him to the couch. Mildred and I sank into the plush armchairs and focused on the introductions to the Eurovision Song Contest. Ever the gentleman, David let us settle into our surroundings before offering drinks.

"White wine," Catherine ordered.

"Cider," Mildred followed.

"Lucozade with ice for me."

He left the room to place the order, and we marveled at our good fortune: a private setting for the greatest show on TV all year long.

"Who would believe this?" I asked Mildred.

"Only you," she grinned. "These things happen only to you."

The song contest was amazing on the giant-size color TV. Mildred and I were enthralled and took no notice of David, though it was hard not to observe that Catherine was working overtime to keep his attention. When all was over and the night still young, he suggested we remove to the residence lounge.

"But I like it here," I protested.

"What about you, Mildred?" he asked.

"I don't care."

"And you?" he asked Catherine.

She jumped to her feet, tossed her long blond hair behind her shoulder, and led the way out of the private room. Not wanting to make a fuss, we simply followed behind. David doubled back to turn off the TV.

The residence lounge was practically empty but for a few men hanging over the bar. Catherine led us to a cozy horseshoe corner nook with an opening on each end. She slid all the way around, followed by Mildred, and then me. Shortly thereafter David marched into the lounge and slid into the seat on my end. I felt a rush of discomfort. Mildred shot me a quizzical look. Catherine appeared unfazed and continued to dominate the conversation. By midnight Mildred and I were fading.

"You know it's really late," I announced. "We should be getting home. I'm really tired."

Mildred looked at her watch and agreed. She nudged Catherine toward the edge, forcing her to slide out of the seat ahead of her. Off they strolled toward the bellboy to reclaim their coats. David took another sip from his drink, deliberately dawdling, letting the girls exit well ahead of us. I was stuck waiting for him to slide out, allowing me freedom. Seeing he had no intention of moving, I began shuffling awkwardly around the booth toward the other exit.

"I'm so sorry," he begged as he leaped to his feet and stretched forward to take my hand.

"Let me help you?"

My heart skipped a beat at his touch. I flushed bright red again. My mouth went dry. I looked for Catherine. She and Mildred had already departed unaware that I was left behind standing like an idiot beside a man who seemed to have no intention of releasing my hand.

"We really need to get going. I'm quite tired and I tend to sleep at the wheel," I blubbered stupidly.

"That's not good," he agreed, now holding my hand with both of his hands like he was about to propose.

"I know, so I better hit the road. Thanks for a wonderful evening. It was amazing seeing the

Eurovision in color on a huge screen. I've never done that before."

"My pleasure. I am only happy to oblige," he responded before whispering, "Can we meet again? Alone."

"Excuse me?" I exclaimed.

"I'd like to spend more time with you."

"But what about Catherine?"

"Ah," he sighed, "your sister is delightful, but you're the one I'm interested in."

I wanted to say, "Can I have my hand back now. I need to go home and think about this." I wanted to say, "Yippee, finally, a man who wants me and not my pretty sister!" I wanted to say, "There must be something wrong with you."

While all these thoughts raced through my head, nothing came out of my mouth.

"What about the same place, same time next week?" he suggested.

"I s'pose," was my feeble reply.

"So, I'll see you here next Saturday at six? Alone!"

"OK."

Recognizing my consternation he gently added, "May I please walk you to your car?"

"Only if you let go of my hand."

He laughed, released my hand, and side-by-side we strolled silently out the hotel door to my car.

En route back to Carndonagh, Mildred and Catherine were instantly asleep, but I was wide-awake revisiting those last few moments over and over again. It messed with my mind all week. I never told Catherine about the hand thing or the date. Bless her dear heart; she couldn't cope with such rejection.

Initially, I enjoyed dating a wealthy hunk of gorgeousness who treated me like a princess. But David was bent on marriage, and I was not. I lay in bed at night agonizing about my inability to commit. What was wrong with me? Why couldn't I be happy with the Pauls, Davids, and Oisíns of this world? They were good men, regular William Darcys. Every woman's dream! And I let them all go, only to continue on the quest for the perfect man, who for all I knew probably didn't exist. I was a romantic at heart and believed in holding out for true love. Settling for less was never an option. One evening David gave me an ultimatum, total commitment or nothing. I chose nothing. I tried to explain to him that my bag of oats was still half full, and I had many more fields to sow. He didn't agree.

"You're not sowing anything. You just don't know what it is you want."

Gabrielle Ní Mheachair

WITHERING ON THE VINE

Over the years, I became more and more dissatisfied with my Donegal life. The loneliness and restlessness failed to abate. Unable to settle, my unhappiness grew daily. Girlfriends were engaged, married, and starting families. Soon I would be a single grape slowly withering on the vine. My pride wouldn't allow that. I had harvested the meadows and failed to find an enchanting prince worthy of me. Truly, I needed fresher more remarkable fodder. Alas, I felt trapped. What sane person leaves a permanent, pensionable government job?

Winifred, my bosom friend, came to me with a question: "Are you going to Greece with the gang this summer?"

"Heck no! Greek men are not my type. A week blistering on the beach is hell, and I hate ouzo. There's nothing for me in Greece. I'll be stuck sightseeing on my own. So, nope, count me out. Not going. Besides I have to work. I've loans to pay off."

"So, are you going back to the bar at the Golflinks Hotel then?"

"Yep, that's the plan."

"I thought you were working there as well?"

"I really want to go visit my Uncle Bill in Boston. He keeps inviting me over, and I was thinking this would be a good summer to go."

"Wow, that's great. We'll miss you in the hotel. It'll be no fun without you."

"Would you come with me? I don't want to go on my own."

"I've no interest in visiting America. America could fall off the planet for all I care."

"But all the girls are going to Greece, and you're the only one left."

"Gee, thanks, I'm your last choice."

"No, you're not, but I assumed you'd be working at the Golflinks."

"I'll be working at the Golflinks for as long as they invite me. What else would I do for the summer?"

Winifred was desperate. She nagged me day and night.

"Fine, I'll think about it."

"You'll have to make your mind up soon, because we need to get visas and book the tickets."

"Oh, God yea. I forgot about that."

Every summer my brother went to New York to earn his college fees. Annually he cajoled and begged me to go with him. Annually I refused. Why would I go to America? I loved my barmaid job at the Golflinks Hotel. Summers in Glengarriff were the highlight of my year, of my life even. Besides,

Mae and Ted, the hotel owners, counted on me to run the bar from the first of June to the first of September. The idea of letting them down was inconceivable. They were my summer parents.

Much to my astonishment, it was Mae who changed my mind. She released me from my commitment and persuaded me to go.

"You're young and free. Go," she insisted. "You might not get the chance again. Besides, the hotel is not going anywhere. You always have a home here."

"Fine, I'll go, but I have conditions," I told Winifred. "We have to work. I'm not spending all my savings on this trip. Also, we have to visit my relatives in New York and my sister in Dallas."

"How are we going to fit all that in?"

"We work six weeks, we travel six weeks."

"Looks like you have it all worked out."

"Well as a matter of fact, I have. We need tickets, visas, and Social Security numbers."

"What are Social Security numbers?"

"We can't work without Social Security numbers."

"How do we get those?"

"Don't worry I have a plan. Right now we need to decide on dates, book the tickets, and get the visas."

As primary teachers with permanent jobs, there was no bother securing a US visitor's visa. Identities were harder to come by, but eventually we secured one male and one female.

"I'm not going to be the boy!" Winifred exclaimed. "You can be Paudi, I'll be Biddy."

"Great. Fine, I'll be Paudi."

Winifred and I were warmly welcomed by her uncle and aunt who invited us to live with them. Within the week we had secured employment as chambermaids at the Boston Warf Hotel. I was Paudi, an Irish form of Patrick, and she was Biddy. Our immediate supervisor, Connie, thought us, "Illiterate Irish Paddies fresh off the boat."

"Can you read?" she asked as she explained how to fill out the supply charts.

"Yea, we can read."

"But can you read English?"

"A little."

"What about writing? Can you write in English?"

"Aye, enough to get by."

She was delighted with that and taught us how to record how many towels we removed from the room, and how many we replaced. At the end of the day, she proudly announced to the other staff, "These Irish girls learn fast."

Connie took great exception to my name, Paudi, which her untrained ear captured as Potty.

"Why would any mother call her child Potty? Do you know what a potty is? You pee in a potty. Imagine calling your child after a potty," she ranted over and over again.

She refused to call me Paudie and re-christened me Pat. Our intellectual ability and strong work ethic speeded up the training period. By day three we had our own carts and floors. At the end of the week Connie called me aside for a wee chat and pointed out that Winifred and I were first to clock out every day.

"That's a good thing, right?"

"No honey, it means you make the rest of us look bad, and you earn less money. You're paid by the hour, you know."

"Oh!"

"You have to clock out by 4 p.m. After that you're not paid."

"So we should just hang around till 4 p.m. and then clock out?"

"Or, you could just take your time."

Henceforth, Winifred and I teamed up, beginning on her floor and finishing on mine. We chatted, took breaks, and dallied until 4 p.m. This priceless advice increased our earnings substantially.

Most of the chambermaids boasted Irish roots and were sincerely inquisitive about the land of their forefathers.

"How did you get to the airport, was it donkey and cart? Was it far for you to travel?"

"Do you have electricity in Ireland yet?"

"It must be terrible to live in Ireland with all the violence."

"Have you ever been shot at?"

"I just love your brogue. Is that what they call Gaelic?"

"Is there still famine in Ireland? All these Irish are still coming over."

"You poor thing, I suppose you have to send every cent home to bring the others over."

"Is it true there are no snakes or mosquitoes in Ireland?"

"How far is it to drive to England?"

Our hotel experience was entertaining, and we grew attached to the staff, who were very kind to us. But when the time came, we had to say goodbye. There were other places to go and people to see. The remaining weeks were spent touring the East Coast from Maine to New York and on down to Dallas. I was particularly stunned at the vastness of America and its extreme diversity. I wanted to see more.

On the plane ride home I asked Winifred, "Well, how was your summer in America?"

"I hated it. I hated every minute of it," was her startling reply.

On further probing, I discovered there was absolutely nothing at all she liked about the United States.

"Well, I had a ball," I confessed guiltily. "I want to return. I'm going to apply for a career break and come back for a year."

"You can do that if you like. I don't care if I never come back. I'm done."

A year later I took the career break, packed my bags and left Donegal. Everyone was convinced I would never return. I had no such convictions, though I was heartily hopeful they were right. I drove through Barnesmore Gap, and Mother's words rang in my ears.

"You're out the gap now, Gabrielle. Off you go and make a life for yourself. There's nothing here for you."

Out the Gap

Made in the USA
Middletown, DE
20 July 2016